Seven Points of Impact

A Compilation
by Linda F. Kluge

7 Points of Impact – A Compilation by Linda F. Kluge

Published by LFK Consulting, LLC
PO Box 888, Bridgeton, MO 63044 USA
Info@7PointsOfImpact.com

Printed in the United States of America
ISBN-978-0-9845315-5-4

Cover Design: Davis Creative, www.DavisCreative.com

Disclaimer

The *7 Points of Impact* book is a compilation/anthology book, containing chapters from 52+ authors. It is designed to provide information and perspectives on the topics of; Spiritual Connection, Life Mission and Purpose, Personal Empowerment, Relationships, Magnificent Mental Mindset, Healthy Bodies Alive to Thrive, and Flourishing Finances. These topics are presented as life coaching options and perspectives, designed to stimulate the creative process of self-directed, selective actions, by reader. The opinions, views and recommendations presented in this book are not necessarily the opinions, views or recommendations of the author Linda F. Kluge or publisher LFK Consulting LLC.

The *7 Points of Impact* book is sold with the understanding that the publisher is not engaged in rendering legal, financial, medical, mental health, psychological counseling or other professional licensed services or advice. The reader is urged to research all available materials on the topics discussed within this book before taking self-directed actions. They are also encouraged to seek professional, medical or legal help as appropriate.

Every effort has been made to accurately represent the coaching style and services offered by each participating author. The reader is urged to fully investigate offerings by any of the participating authors before securing services.

The author and publisher shall have neither liability nor responsibility to any person or entity with respect to any loss or damage caused, or alleged to have been caused, directly or indirectly, by the information contained in this book.

Book Orders
Visit the 7 Points of Impact Site to order books
www.7PointsOfImpact.com

To

All that we are...

And, all we may become...

This book is dedicated to the reader

For having the courage to consider diverse perspectives

Having the faith to implement life-affirming transformational changes

May Your

Life Be

Evergreen!

Acknowledgments

As the Project Coordinator for the 7 Points of Impact anthology book, I would like to express my sincere gratitude to the many people who supported me in bringing this endeavor to fruition:

To my family and friends who are the golden thread in my life

The 7 Pts planning team: Kathy Wasserman, Cathy Davis, Kelly Alcorn and Dave Schwent

The 52 authors for their willingness to make a bold statement in the world

Sandra Yancey and the corporate staff at the e-WomenNetwork, Dallas TX

Jack & Cathy Davis, Davis Creative for layout support and cover creation

Karen Garcia for editing and creative talents

Rev. Pat Powers for her creative input and loving support

Karen Hoffman, Patty Cook and the Joy of Goals

Every member of YCB - Your Collaborative Board, St. Louis, MO

Donna Gamache and e-WomenNetwork St. Louis, MO

Powerful You Women's Network, St. Louis, MO

Christine Kloser and Conscious Entrepreneurs for leading the way

Milana Leshinsky for Recurring Revenue Revolution training

Jaimes McNeal and Phoenix Arises Seminars, St. Louis, MO

Michal Abney and the BreakThrough movie

To CallKayla.com for the 7 Points of Impact web site

Karen Drucker for your songs of inspiration and an unforgettable retreat in Tahoe.

To the Gateway to Agape Choir...you help my spirit soar!

Brynn T. Palmer who selflessly sponsored one of our authors

Sue Schneider who has made an incredible impact in my own life

Sincere & Enduring Gratitude, *Linda F. Kluge*

Contents

Personal Empowerment

Relationships

Magnificent Mental Mindset

Healthy Bodies Alive to Thrive

Flourishing Finances

Introduction

By Linda F. Kluge

Welcome to the *7 Points of Impact* perspectives!

This anthology book contains chapters from more than 52 contributing authors. It is designed to provide inspiration, information and perspectives on the life topics of:

- Spiritual Connection
- Life Mission and Purpose
- Personal Empowerment
- Relationships
- Magnificent Mental Mindset
- Healthy Bodies Alive to Thrive
- Flourishing Finances

The discussions on these topics are presented as life-coaching options, transformational tools and individual viewpoints designed to stimulate the creative process of self-directed, selective actions by readers. One small shift can change your life. Better choices lead to improved results.

The *7 Points of Impact* book was born from the desire to be helpful to others. Every moment we are born anew. Life is ever changing, ever evolving. Some changes are self-orchestrated, while others come to our lives through a series of events or life circumstances seemingly beyond our realm of influence. Yet, each person holds the capabilities to move or change with the ever-shifting tides of life...even if we only adjust our own perspectives.

Compiling the *7 Points of Impact* book has been one of the most rewarding collaborative projects I have ever been privileged to be a part of. The inception of the 7 Points concept came from my desire to lead a balanced life and my own writings on that topic. The true blessing occurred as I began to "attract the right and perfect authors" into this project. What a privilege it has been to work with, and be in a relationship with, this magnificent group of ministers, mentors, coaches and entrepreneurs.

I believe a more powerful force, a Higher Power, supported me in my ability to attract authors who are strong, independent thinkers longing to have a positive impact on the world. The same energetic, loving, guiding force will now attract the "right and perfect readers" to this book and into our lives.

It is our sincere desire that these diverse perspectives touch your heart, inspire you and open new, life-changing possibilities for you. Let the words in these chapters illuminate the path as you seek your truth. Be your authentic self...true to that which brings the highest and best to your life. We also encourage you to remember this paradox:

You are perfect the way you are...
So is your desire to change!

Serenity Prayer

God Grant Me the Serenity

To Accept the Things I Cannot Change...

Courage to Change the Things I Can...

And the Wisdom to

Know the Difference!

Seven Points of Impact

Point

1

Spiritual Connection

About the Author

 With a background in accounting and a long career in business management, Sharon Kohler shared her experience and expertise with the US Peace Corps as an older volunteer. Originally recruited as one of the first hundred business advisors to Russia, but unexpectedly sidetracked by emergency surgery, she was assigned, instead, to the Kingdom of Tonga in the South Pacific.

Working with the Tonga Development Bank, Sharon set ambitious goals and worked towards those objectives with flexibility and determination. She is credited with being the driving force behind the first South Pacific Regional Business Conference (SPRBC), sponsored by both the Peace Corps and the Tonga Development Bank. The conference brought together forty Small Business Advisors from throughout the Pacific and resulted in the implementation of such programs as Junior Achievement and Start Your Own Business, Improve Your Own Business (SYOB/IYOB) in many developing countries. Such a conference had been proposed for years, but Sharon's resolve and consensus-building talents made it happen. As a measure of her professional standing with the Bank, she was selected to travel to the participating countries to perform the needs assessment that served as the prelude to the SPRBC. She was also selected by her fellow volunteers to be their representative at a Non-Formal Education Workshop in West Samoa and an All Volunteer Agency Conference in Fiji. To be selected twice for positions of such responsibility is an honor never before given to a volunteer. Her organizational skills, sound judgment and capable leadership hallmark her exciting career.

God's Promise

By Sharon Kohler

My job of ten years was ending when a friend said to me, "I know what your plans are...you'll probably work a few more years, save a little more money, retire, and then join the Peace Corps."

"Peace Corps?" I asked. "I haven't thought about the Peace Corps in years! They wouldn't be interested in a fifty year old woman." At his urging, I phoned 800-information and requested the number for the Peace Corps. I was totally unprepared for their interest in a woman of my age and background.

For most of my career I had worked in business administration, most recently as the general manager and controller for one of the most successful commercial office furniture dealerships in the Southeast. As I began to explore the Peace Corps application process, I kept asking myself if I was being foolish to even consider leaving my family for two plus years to become an older volunteer in a remote part of the world. I had an aging mother and two children who were trying to start their families. My daughter, Amy, had suffered several devastating miscarriages, one very recently; and my son Rick and his wife were also hoping to have a child.

As the Peace Corps' interest in me grew, my doubts and misgivings kept pace. There were many, many sleepless nights while I made lists of the pros and cons, looking at all the possible consequences and agonizing over my decision. My health began to suffer, and I finally realized I should take it to God in prayer. After all, my faith had taught me to do this; and yet it was my last step in the decision process. I now realize it should have been my first!

I knelt and prayed sincerely to God for help with this decision. Suddenly, I felt a calm and peace that is very difficult to describe; and a deep, comforting voice spoke to me, ***"Go and do this! It is a good thing. You will be safe and so will your loved ones. You have my word. You have my promise."*** A spiritual connection had been made, and it would be tested and then validated in the most astounding way.

From that moment on, it became clear that I could and should accept the Peace Corps' assignment to the Kingdom of Tonga, a little island nation in the middle of the South Pacific. I sold my dream home in the suburbs, placed everything I owned in storage and, with complete confidence and the full blessing of my family, set off on the most exciting adventure of my life!

I was fearless. Tonga is a Polynesian country comprised of 174 islands, with only 34 of them inhabited. My host-country counterpart, Mosese, and I traveled to the outer islands teaching standard accounting practices, such as simple bookkeeping and inventory control, to the small business people of these islands. At times we would be in a small wooden boat about to cross the deepest part of the Pacific Ocean, the Tongan Trench, without life jackets. Even with the boat sitting so low in the water that there was only a foot of "freeboard" showing, I would still cheerfully call, "We have room for one more". The bugs, the tiny airplanes that would take us to the furthest islands, the "scary" sleeping places, and all the other challenges that face any Peace Corps volunteer in a developing nation, held no undue fear or concern for me. I felt completely sheltered and protected...and I loved it! It was a dream come true. I wouldn't trade one moment of it.

I could relish and enjoy every exotic experience...from traveling with the King of Tonga to claim and name a new island forming from a still-erupting volcano deep under the ocean, to sitting with a friend on the beach of an uninhabited island, eating raw tuna that had just been caught...without the background fears that sometimes dim our joy and tarnish the moment.

Once, when stranded on a small island with a runway that stretched from one side of the island to the other and a plane propeller that would not "catch", I wondered *how long* before we would be able to leave, *not would we make it*. A Tongan stood on the top of a pick-up truck and installed a "modified" engine part. The pilot asked the eight of us who waited under the nearest coconut tree to re-board the plane. His plan was to taxi to the end of the runway, turn around and taxi as fast as possible to the other end of the runway. He said he thought that speed would help start the propeller. It was very quiet as we gained speed, and the ocean at the end of the runway came closer and closer. The propeller "caught," we lifted off, made a slow turn and headed for the next island. Mosese and the others exhaled and slumped in relief. I smiled...I knew we would be okay!

During this time, my mother's health stayed amazingly good; and she even spent six weeks with me. For the first time in her life, she traveled alone outside of the United States, flying more than 10,000 miles. She loved Tonga; and we spent three weeks visiting New Zealand, all the while creating memories that will last our lifetime. Fifteen years later, we still reminisce about this time together. Also, while I was away, my son and daughter each gave me a new granddaughter...perfect pregnancies with perfect results. How awesome!

At the end of my Peace Corps service, I followed the example of many volunteers and traded my ticket home for an around the world ticket. Traveling west and spending weeks in each spot, I made my way through Australia, Indonesia, and Thailand. At the beginning of my second month in Thailand, my daughter contacted me in Bangkok with an urgent message. My eighteen month old granddaughter, Taylor, had been in an accident and suffered a broken femur. She was in a full body cast, and I was needed to help care for her.

Flying for 48 hours straight, I arrived in Los Angeles, exhausted and in need of a restroom. As I hurried down the concourse, looking for the facilities, I was suddenly blinded by a bright light in my eyes. It came from inside a gift shop, and it was persistent... if I moved my head, it followed. I was compelled to turn into the shop to see what it was. It led me straight to a revolving stand on a jewelry counter. The brilliance was coming from a key chain that had a round gold disk attached. The disk said *"God Keeps His Promises"*. For an instant, the world stopped for me. I felt humbled and awed as I realized that the moment I stepped on American soil, not only had He reminded me of His promise, He had validated our spiritual connection.

To this day, I become emotional when talking about this experience. Clearly, I was blessed with a direct message from God. He had watched over us and kept my family and me safe. He had also given me purpose, both in undertaking a commitment with the Peace Corps and in returning to care for Taylor, who, by the way, healed completely with no memory of her time in a body cast.

The power of prayer is undeniable! Spiritual connections are real! I am eternally grateful for this life lesson and for every wonderful moment of my time in the Peace Corps. I am also grateful for any opportunity to share my story, as it is my witness to God for His many blessings to me.

Footnote: The Peace Corps is still alive and playing a vital role in the world today. They welcome older volunteers and their valuable contributions of life-experience and expertise. The Peace Corps can be reached at 1-800 424-8580. My advice is to pray first and then call. Incidentally, I purchased the keychain that morning in Los Angeles; and for the rest of my life I will carry no other.

*****

In 2011 the Peace Corps will commemorate 50 years of promoting peace and friendship around the world. The agency's mission and legacy of service is honored by past volunteers like Sharon Kohler, demonstrating the effectiveness of Peace Corps programs and inspiring the next generation of volunteers through education and engagement. www.PeaceCorps.gov

About the Author

 Rev. Marigene DeRusha has been a Minister and Spiritual Director since graduating from the ministerial program at the Northwest College for Holistic Studies in Seattle, Washington, in 1983. She is committed to serving others in love and joy. Her purpose here on planet Earth is: "To celebrate the connection of Life, to ignite the spark of Divinity, to evoke the passion of Creativity, and to assist people on their Spiritual journeys".

Marigene became the minister at the Center for Spiritual Living in St. Louis, Missouri, in 2003 after 20 years in the ministry. She brings joy, love and storytelling to the spiritual community she so lovingly serves. Marigene often reminds us, "We are a blessing to the Universe...Live in Love!"

You may connect with Rev. Marigene at the Center for Spiritual Living, Saint Louis, Missouri (www.stlouis-csl.org), a place to dig deeper into your spiritual studies and "Practice the Presence" daily in your spiritual life. The United Centers for Spiritual Living national headquarters can direct you to a center in your geographic region: (www.UnitedCentersForSpiritualLiving.org).

Connection to Spirit

By Rev. Marigene DeRusha

My life changed profoundly in 1963 as I was entering my senior year of high school. I was sixteen years old, and my parents took my siblings and me on a road trip to San Francisco to visit my oldest brother. We decided to visit the Teton Mountains on the way. I was sitting on a boulder looking out at the mountain when all of a sudden everything around me disappeared. It became very, very quiet...the only thing I was aware of was a oneness with the mountain. There was no "me" anymore. I had only a sense of love, oneness and power. I sat with my expanded self of energy just 'being' the mountain until finally I heard my mother telling us to get back into the car. I asked my siblings about that awesome experience; and they all thought I was crazy, as they didn't notice anything different. I knew that life was more than I had been taught or realized. I knew there was a Oneness of all life, and there was no beginning and no ending to me.

After marrying young and having two children, I discovered a whole branch of information known as metaphysics. It began for me with discovering Edgar Cayce and his writings. As I began my quest of learning in my 20's, I realized that Spirituality is the search to know our true selves. I never knew I had a 'true self' from studying religion. I began to understand my experience of Oneness at the Mountain. Growing up in a Roman Catholic home and school, I had never heard the term, "spiritual". I had heard about "religion". I just thought there were rules and dogma that one followed with little say in how it affected my life. I prayed to "a-God-out-there" that may have heard me. He was sort of like a big Santa Claus, living mysteriously somewhere in the sky, detached from me, and sometimes granting wishes/prayers... sometimes not.

In 1969 I was connected again with this "One Energy" that I had experienced in the Teton Mountains. Another introduction to a new way of being changed my life! I was a single mom raising two children and decided to spend the night at my parents' home. I woke up in the middle of the night, and the wall to the outside front yard had dissolved completely. I was sitting in bed looking at the tree across the street! I was thinking, "Where is the wall, and how did it disappear?" I noticed that I could see the veins on each leaf on the tree across the street, even though I wasn't wearing my glasses and am practically blind without them. There was no wall anymore, just this amazing energy.

I could feel "an Energy of Love" enveloping me and the whole room. I heard from within, "never worry, everything is unfolding perfectly; and you are love and loved." I was so content knowing there was more and all was okay that I promptly went back to sleep.

That was over thirty years ago, and I still remember the feeling of love and peace and knowing that all is well. It was after this experience that I became so committed to my spiritual journey. I wanted to learn more and experience more. I read everything I could about metaphysics, life after death, the journey of the self; and I began a meditation practice.

We have a choice as to the life we want to live. The choice is the "inner life"...our thoughts, beliefs, attitudes, and intentions that create our outer world. What "story" about life are you focusing on? Does it bring pleasure or suffering? The suffering keeps us stuck in the past or fear of the future. If we live in the moment and just breathe, we can connect with this Presence within.

I find that when I think I am "my story" that I am telling, I don't live from the essence of who I am. I love what Byran Katie taught me: "There is my business, your business, and God's business". I find that if I am stuck in your business, who is tending to my business? It may be hard to let go of our "stories" about how life "should" or "could be" or "has been". We stay in the past or the future with our stories and miss the beauty and the experience of the "Now Moment".

To connect to the Divine Spirit within is the path of spirituality. It is the act of getting to know yourself so totally that you surrender everything to the process of "going inside" to discover the "Oneness" that you are. The Universe is always giving us opportunities. We can let go of the past or stay stuck. What feels the best? Is it peace you want or suffering? Do you want to feel heavy or light hearted?

I am not the stories I told you about my life; but those stories opened my eyes to a Universe without form, a connected Universe that is calling us to know we are love. If we hold onto a story of misery, we won't get to the place of love; in fact, we will stay stuck in the past with misery. Make your story one of expansion, Oneness, a dance with the Divine.

As I began my "Quest of Spirit" years ago, I realized that Spirituality is the search to know our true selves. We are all spiritual beings who are here on planet Earth to love and learn from our experiences of life and what we choose to focus our attention on. This Divine Intelligence uses us for greater good, when we pay attention! Sometimes we get stuck in our ego, "Edging God Out," and act as if we aren't inner-connected and part of the whole. Although our thoughts, feelings and personalities may vary considerably, the essence of who we are remains the same. We are each a very different person than we were ten years ago or ten days ago, but still we feel the same sense of "Oneness". This sense of "Oneness" is the same for everyone and, in that respect, is something universal that we all share. This Divine Wisdom responds as we allow it to guide us toward greater good.

Most spiritual teachings also maintain that when one comes to know the true nature of consciousness, one also comes to know God. If this Divine Intelligence is the essence of the whole of creation, then this Divine Intelligence has to be the essential essence of every creature and every person. This is why the search to discover the nature of one's own innermost essence is the search for our Higher Power.

Developing a Spiritual Practice is essential to the inner connection of life and our awareness that sets us free. How do we access our spirituality? We have to enter into the silence and know that all is Divine Intelligence. That is the first step.

The essence of spirituality is the search to know our true selves, to discover the real nature of consciousness. This quest has been the foundation of all the great spiritual teachings, and the goal of all the great mystics.

Spirituality Can Be...

- The Search for a Higher Power
- Search for Greater Connectivity, Meaning, Understanding
- A Journey of Self-Discovery...Within the Concept of Connectedness
- Questioning Current Beliefs with Open Mindedness
- Appreciating the Awe and Wonder of it All

Why should we develop our spirituality?

So, what are the benefits of spirituality? This inner journey has a direct relationship to the outer journey. It can offer benefits mentally, emotionally and physically. It can bring a sense of greater purpose while helping you understand your passions professionally, socially, and personally. Several studies show positive beliefs such as, comfort, a greater sense of peace and improved health show up in your life. Go deeper with Spirit and live the Divine Dance!

Stay in Communion with the Divine...
and allow your life to unfold perfectly!

About the Author

 Karen Hoffman is "Your Dream Champion" (www.YourDreamChampion.com) and loves to Ignite Possibilities through Connections and Collaboration.

When Karen was featured in St. Louis Magazine, she was called "The Queen of Possibilities". As an author, speaker and multi-prenuer, Karen thrives on helping entrepreneurs (particularly women) succeed and achieve. She believes that "new possibilities always exist" and that "hope ignites us into action".

Through City of Experts (www.CityofExperts.com) she loves to promote expert speakers and consultants. Her unique program, Joy of Goals, helps people vision, dream, connect and collaborate towards the achievement of their objectives (www.JoyofGoals. com). Her most recent venture is Gateway to Dreams (www. GatewaytoDreams.org) which pulls the community together to dream, connect and collaborate.

It is no wonder that Karen has been the recipient of a multitude of awards including: eWomen Network International's "Business Matchmaker of the Year"; the Regional Commerce & Growth Association's "Pacesetter Award"; the SBA's "Home-Based Business Champion"; and Zonta International's "Yellow Rose" Humanitarian Assistance Award for Empowering and Supporting Women.

Her book "The Art of Barter – How to Trade for Almost Anything" was released in April, 2010 and is available online or at local bookstores.

"The Voice"

By Karen Hoffman

There are two ways to live your life —
one is as though nothing is a miracle,
the other is as though everything is a miracle.
Albert Einstein

Have you ever had an intuitive prompting or heard a voice in your head and wondered...was it you talking to you or something more? The longer I live the more I'm learning that it is something more...something miraculous moving in our lives.

I'll admit to you right now, my mind is a noisy place. I hear the voice of my own conscious thoughts, my subconscious awareness and a voice I have come to rely on as my inner guidance system. To me, this is the voice of God (or to some, perhaps, better explained as the voice of Spirit).

It has taken me several decades to: (1) admit to myself that I hear voices and (2) admit to others that I hear voices. It was in 1997, though, when something happened that helped me open up to the voices and conversations I have with myself...and with God.

Some of you reading this will say, "That isn't new! I KNOW those voices!" But there are some of you who might not experience intuitive promptings in this same manner. I hope by sharing my story with you that you might not wait as long as I did to entertain...and yes, embrace...the possibility that God communicates with all of us in many ways. I hope, as well, that on your spiritual journey you might become even more tuned in to the guidance, as I have.

It was in 1997 that "the voice" became something for which I was incredibly thankful. The voice of God/Spirit has probably been with me since birth; however, until 1997, I mostly denied it, calling it coincidences or sometimes even angels.

What happened that impacted me so dramatically that I now have the courage to share my stories? Let me take you back to 1996. Sometime that year, I started having pain during intimacy with my husband. When I visited my ob-gyn, he dismissed it as an infection...a misdiagnosis that could have proved fatal.

Multiple rounds of antibiotics were prescribed, but the problem did not subside. Over the course of that year, it was a painful nuisance and something I started to think I would just have to learn to live with. But then, in December 1996, I was again visiting the ob-gyn's office and (due to my regular doctor's retirement) was sharing my concerns with his former partner. In looking at my file, he said that he felt the regimen of antibiotics would have cleared up any infection and that perhaps it was fibroids. He also suggested that I might want to consider a partial hysterectomy. They would preserve my ovaries and remove any fibroid tumors that might be contributing to my discomfort.

When I asked about the downsides, the doctor said I would no longer have menstrual periods. At age 43, this did not seem like a downside at all, but actually a cool benefit! No more "time of the month"? No more pain during intercourse? Keep my ovaries?

Hormone production stays intact? This was starting to sound like a great plan to me!

But when would we do it? The doctor said it was "elective", not an emergency, so I could plan it at a time that was convenient for me. He told me I would need to take it easy for four to six weeks, so I reviewed my work schedule and decided that summer would be an ideal time. I envisioned working part time (I love working) and "taking it easy". Taking it easy meant I'd take paperwork outside and get fresh air and sun...get a nice tan. Being part Arawak Indian (my father was from South America), tans come easily; and I'd not had a nice tan in years. Yes, I know the dangers; but for this one summer I was going to kick back and have a nice tan. My plan was mapped out!

However...almost immediately...I started hearing this voice, which I later came to believe was the voice of God/Spirit. The voice objected to the summer surgery and insisted I should "get it over with". That was the refrain I kept hearing..."Get it over with."

"Get it over with."

I objected, "Not until summer! My plan! My tan"! At times, I must confess, I felt a little foolish arguing with this voice; and I WAS arguing with this voice! Sometimes I found myself even raising my own voice in my head to try and drown out the "get it over with" refrain. "No! I want to wait for summer!"

But the intuitive promptings were too strong.

"Okay! I'll get it over with!" I then called and arranged surgery for the second week in February (certainly a far cry from summer in the Midwest).

So, there it was. Surgery set...the plan for a tan derailed, and I was feeling less than enthusiastic!

On the day of the surgery, my husband escorted me and was going to wait for me during the partial hysterectomy. As I was prepped, I was given a standard form to sign. Since all surgeries come with possible dangers, I was asked to sign a form that gave them permission to remove my ovaries if they found any unusual growths or cancer. I remember objecting because that was NOT part of the projected plan. However, my doctor came out, told me it was a "formality" and that I should sign it. According to him, there was no indication that there were any signs of cancer, so I did sign it; and then I was sent up for surgery.

When I woke up hours later, I saw my husband sitting by my side with a strange look on his face. His look was so serious, like his pet dog had died or something, so I asked him what was wrong. He looked at me, still with this strange look. He asked me, kind of shocked, "They didn't tell you?"

"Tell me what?" I wondered in my semi-dazed state. Then I said it out loud. Hesitating, he said the word that changes everything: "Cancer". At this point, I'm coherent enough to know I went in there for a partial hysterectomy, NOT for anything REMOTELY connected to "cancer". So I tell him to stop kidding around and tell me what was going on.

He says again, with a pleading tone, "They didn't tell you?"

Now I'm starting to get that he is not kidding. From the time I went in for surgery and up to the time I came out, something in my world had changed radically. Cancer? Me?

Yes...it was true. My doctor came in later and proceeded to tell me that, yes, it was ovarian cancer. They were waiting for test results, but an oncology gynecologist had come in to surgery to remove the cancer and ovaries.

That voice telling me to "Get it over with"...was that God talking to me? I believe so. As it was, I was diagnosed with stage 3 ovarian cancer in 1997. I went through chemotherapy; and as I write this, in 2010, I am still standing here, cancer free, thanks to my willingness to listen to that voice! I now have no doubt that I heard God...and I am now a better listener.

About the Author

 Rev. Cindy Middendorf is the founder and director of Spirit Connection, a non-profit ministry whose purpose is to assist in healing all barriers to relationships with God, self, others, family and community. She seeks to feed the hearts, souls, minds and bodies of the people she serves. She promotes healthy spiritual living through her work with Spirit Connection (www. Spirit-Connection.net) and physical wellness through nutrient-rich Xocai™ healthy chocolate (www.ThreeChocolatesADay.com).

Making the Spiritual Connection

By Rev. Cindy Middendorf

Looking back through history, we can see that we humans have always had a belief, an intuition, a real sense of our connection, to a higher power...a deeper meaning. We want our lives to have real purpose and meaning. We want to be happy. Many of us have religious affiliations. Often our religious beliefs have been handed down to us through family ancestry and traditions or we have adopted the belief systems of those who were important and influential in our lives. Whatever our religious experience or lack thereof, we have spiritual needs and yearnings.

Spirituality is different from religion. A religion is generally a set of beliefs regarding the worship of a god or gods and the origin of the universe. Religious organizations provide a structure and context for that worship and the expression of those beliefs. Spirituality, on the other hand, is a transcendent reality of the world that stems from a person's inner path to discover the essence of their own being. An individual's personal spirituality has a lot to do with the deep meanings and values that guide how we live and the choices we make.

Although religious beliefs and practices are an integral part of spirituality for many people, a person can be deeply spiritual without being religious. I consider Mother Theresa to be a great example of someone who was deeply spiritual and also very religious. Young peacemaker, poet and philosopher, Mattie Stepanek (1990-2004) inspired millions from his wheelchair through his motivational speaking and his best-selling books[1] about "Heartsongs". He was certainly very spiritual without promoting any particular religion. Whether or not you are religious, it is important to know, embrace, and cultivate your own spirituality.

When I was a little girl growing up on a Midwest farm, I would wander down the dirt road behind the big barn out into the open fields. There was a huge tree there that I called "the God tree". I would sit in the lush grass under the God tree and stare out across the open plain with wonder and awe. I would smell the freshness of the air and feel gentle breezes against my skin. The soft texture of the grass over the solid earth beneath me gave me a feeling of gentle support. I would gaze into the vast open sky and just admire the beauty of it. Here, I felt very connected. It was a spiritual connection. Even now, decades later, I can feel that connection just by remembering my time under the God tree. By recalling the details and feelings of those experiences, I provide myself with the perfect mental equivalent of actually having the experience.

As a young woman, I was very involved with getting an education, having a career, making a home with my husband and raising our children. I had an active religious life and was very involved with my faith community. When I was in my mid-twenties, my father died. Up until that time, I had a lot of unanswered spiritual questions that I pushed aside and ignored; but my grief and anger at losing my father made those questions louder and

---

[1] Mattie J.T. Stepanek, *Heartsongs, Journey Through Heartsongs, Hope Through Heartsongs, Celebrate Through Heartsongs, Loving Through Heartsongs, Reflections of a Peacemaker, and Just Peace: A Message of Hope.*

louder in my mind and heart. This led to a spiritual crisis for me. I had to find answers. I did some serious soul-searching, seeking, studying and exploring. I came to understand my own spirituality in a deeper and more meaningful way. For me, it led to moving away from the religion in which I had grown up to find one that served my needs in a much greater way. I came to understand that I am a spiritual being having a human experience.

Over the years, I have also come to understand myself as a whole being with a spiritual, mental, emotional, intellectual, physical and relational reality. I know these are all intertwined and connected. They don't exist in isolation from each other. Stress in our mental and/or emotional experience results in effects in our physical body experience. Only in recent years has there been much study about the mind-body connection, although it seems that this was always evident in the ancient wisdom of humanity.

We are always at a choice, whether we recognize it or not. When we stand in any question, failure to make a choice is actually a choice. In religious terms, many people think of this as Free Will. We human beings have the unique gift of self awareness or self-consciousness. We recognize ourselves as thinking, breathing, loving beings and are capable of self-contemplation and self-improvement. We have the ability to recognize those situations that "push our buttons" and/or trigger old memories that we do not like, and we can choose to change our response. Rather than react out of habit, we can respond with ability, i.e., take responsibility for our own happiness and welfare.

So what does it mean to make a spiritual connection? A spiritual connection occurs when we are in tune with our inner divine nature, when we feel connected to the whole, the Greater Reality of life. For each person this is different. Some people require quiet contemplative time to feel connected, while others resonate more with intense physical activities, such as running or dancing.

When I sit on my porch swing and listen to the birds sing, feel the breeze, and observe the sky and trees, I am making a spiritual connection. Vast, open, powerful spaces in nature are the places I feel most connected, just like I felt under the God tree when I was a little girl. Just remembering such moments can allow us to use the perfect mental equivalent of that experience to create the spiritual connection right now in this moment.

While I feel connected in wide open spaces, others may feel more connected in a snug, cozy place next to a toasty fire. Still others find the best solace soaking in a tub of warm, pleasing water. Others may want to move to the beat of a drum, chant, sing, or dance. Whatever soothes your soul, makes you feel supported and loved, and brings you a felt sense of belonging, is a way for you to be spiritually connected.

Meditation is a wonderful way to make a spiritual connection. There are many techniques for meditation, but the purpose of all meditation is to slow down and become mindful of the silence that exists. Think of it as the silence between thoughts. Our goal in meditation is to expand the silence between thoughts. This allows us to be at peace, to be open and receptive to receiving intuition or divine guidance, and to let go of that unimportant, but all-consuming, busyness of modern life we have created.

Prayer, chanting, singing and reading aloud from sacred texts or inspirational materials are also great spiritual practices to bring us into a feeling of connection with God, the Universe or higher power...or however you perceive the Greater Reality, that which is beyond the physical. Many people like to use affirmations or declarations to direct their thinking and feeling nature toward the good they desire for their lives. An example might be saying aloud to oneself, "I am a prosperous being living in an abundant Universe. Everything I need is already mine".

Gratitude is also an amazingly powerful spiritual practice. Many spiritual teachers promote keeping a daily gratitude journal. I personally like to start every day with gratitude. Before I step out of bed, I list for myself three things I am grateful to have and three things I am grateful to be. This also helps me to maintain a positive attitude about myself and how I am showing up in the world.

Whatever calls to you from within, take time to listen and seek the deeper meaning in your own life. If you don't already have spiritual practices that serve you well, experiment and find what brings you that spiritual connection. Your search will undoubtedly be very rewarding.

About the Author

 Dorris Burch believes an exciting, meaningful, and intentional life awaits every woman as she learns how to live beyond fear and begins living boldly. Through the Proverbs 31 Women Experience ~ The Enterprising Business Woman ~ Institute for Entrepreneurial Learning, Dorris coaches her clients to be heart-centered visionaries. By changing their mindsets and enabling women to realize their inherent worth, she guides them to discover their 'light', which links what women are to what they can be. Dorris continues to create courses, events and mentoring programs to assist women in achieving their dreams quicker and with less effort than they thought possible. For more information, go to: www.proverbs31womanexperience.com.

Designed To Be Brilliant

Unleash Your Presence – Your Power – Your Passion

By Dorris Burch

There is a power within—a fountain of unlimited resources—and she who controls her power controls circumstances instead of circumstances controlling her.

Within every woman there is a powerful force filled with passion, creativity, and ageless knowing. Once a woman has regained her purpose and destiny, her creative life blossoms; and she begins to grow and thrive. Without your purpose and destiny, you forget why you're here...to enrich the lives of others.

I love Jeremiah 29:11 (Msg Bible) *"I know what I'm doing. I have it all planned out—plans to take care of you, not abandon you, plans to give you the future you hope for."*

Amazing that God's plan for me has always been bigger and better than the one I had for me! This is where DESIGNED TO BE BRILLIANT comes into play.

Woman are born gifted; and when you are not in your purpose and destiny, you feel stuck, fatigued, uncreative, weak, depressed, powerless, unable to follow through, without soulfulness, without meaning. You make life-sapping choices in mates, work and friendships. When you lose touch with your instinctive purpose and destiny, you live in a semi-destroyed state. This is why being in your purpose and destiny is utterly essential to your mental and soul health.

Instead Of Living Freely, You Are Living Falsely
As women, we still often feel less than adequate. We are insecure
when we are not confident. This has everything to do with how
we see ourselves. Most of the time, the way we see ourselves
is based on the way we think others see us, which can be all
consuming. When we feel insignificant, lesser than or doubt
our worth, this affects how we relate to others and the way we
view ourselves. As long as we are forced into believing we are
rendered powerless by circumstances, we are living less, rather
than living more.

Unfortunately, most women don't believe they were DESIGNED
TO BE BRILLIANT. Even if we say we believe it, we don't live as
if we do. Why do I say this? Well, we say we believe this, yet we
do things that contradict what we say we believe. If we really
believe we were DESIGNED TO BE BRILLIANT, why are we
constantly comparing ourselves to others...wishing we had their
money, their successful businesses, their looks, their bodies, their
clothes, and their lives?

The only way to stop this insecurity is to live out the truth of
who you are. You begin to release the hold that insecurity has
on you by being crystal clear about what you are insecure about,
accepting that you "made it all up" in your mind. It is a lie that
you've told yourself for years. It is your responsibility to cancel
the lie and start to build your self-worth, shifting your mental
focus to the truth inside of you to believe that you really are
DESIGNED TO BE BRILLIANT.

The most universal and inescapable law there is, is the law of cause and effect. Where there is a cause, there must be an effect; where there is an effect, there must have been a cause.

The world of appearances has a "hold" over our minds. We totally accept appearances as all there is, and we are victims to it all. Why? Because we accept it as the only reality, and the bonds in our lives are mental. When you take an honest survey of your life, you most often find that you have been the one allowing your dreams, goals and hopes to be destroyed.

When you get this fully...then you are free to live the full, successful, satisfying life that God meant for you to live.

Choose To Be On A Mission
DESIGNED TO BE BRILLIANT is about the pursuit of being the woman you were created to be. It is discovering that light inside of you that carries your dreams and goals. The only way to transform your dreams and goals is the pursuit. This is the master key that unlocks all of life's possibilities. The world makes room for a woman on a pursuit. Successful lives are motivated by dynamic pursuit. Once you get your dream going, you have to maintain its momentum.

You already have been given what you need to begin to create your future. Your opportunity is right where you are now. You should do what it takes to get out of your comfort zone. Let go of your fear. Let go of resistance.

Are you letting outward appearances, other people's opinions or statistics rule your business...or more importantly, your mind? Your mind is your world. When you rule your mind, you rule your world. Beneath the chaos of our lives lies a divine purpose and perfect plan. Starting today, you can do something about it! The past does not exist for you anymore, except in your mind. You can erase past mistakes, guilt, failures and fear from the chalkboard of your mind. Remove false and limited beliefs that you yourself have invented.

Unleash Your Purpose and Live Life to Its Max!

"When you discover your mission, you will feel its demand. It will fill you with enthusiasm and a burning desire to get to work on it."

– W. Clement Stone

Each of us is a unique creation, drawn to this particular place in life, at this particular time. It is when you discover Truth for yourself, when you realize that you are a spiritual being having a human experience, that you really begin to live. You do not fit into a mold; rather, you have your own pattern to unfold, your own destiny to fulfill, your own reason for being, your own place in God's perfect scheme of things.

The potential for greatness that is in you surpasses anything I can envision for you. But I know that you were sent forth to unleash your purpose. This is your spiritual awakening in which the light begins to shine in you and for you. It's your knowledge of the soul to fulfill out in the world. You will begin to live knowing that you have a self of that has grown in ways you cannot imagine; you have a self that stands glorious and free.

As we open our minds, hearts and lives to light and guidance, we are shown what is right and essential for us to do. We are given the wisdom and the strength to say no to those things that we now see as time-consuming, but not important or needful. You are needed, you are important, you are worthy; you have your own place to fill in this world. You are a unique, important creation of God. God always has been the source of your supply. His supply has many channels through which it manifests itself. God's supply is not limited.

Let your authenticity shine. You are a one-of-a-kind woman with a distinct personality, unique gifts, and the potential to make a mark in this world that is different from any other. When you know that you were DESIGNED TO BE BRILLIANT, you look at the world differently. Instead of seeing roadblocks, you know there are no limits to what you can accomplish, except the limits you place on yourself.

DESIGNED TO BE BRILLIANT enables ordinary women, like you and me, to live with higher and greater expectancies to become extraordinary and legendary, using our passions and skills to make an unimaginable impact on the world. God wants to do more than you can even ask or think of; but remember, it's according to the power that works in you.

It's time to stand out!

About the Author

 Rev. Pat Powers, a native of the St. Louis Metropolitan area, holds a Masters of Arts in Consciousness Studies and is an Ordained Minister with United Centers for Spiritual Living. Rev. Pat teaches a powerful, positive-thinking spiritual philosophy to the seeker, the "Cultural Creatives", who are looking for love, inspiration, fulfillment, career coaching, and defining life purpose towards the objective of creating a better life...a better world.

Rev. Pat offers individual spiritual coaching, couples counseling, facilitates workshops and weekend intensives, teaches group classes, gives keynote presentations and speaks to groups both large and small. Her efforts as a master of ceremonies, fundraiser and lively auctioneer have helped raise significant contributions for local, regional, national and international charities.

She serves as a Chaplain at Alternative Hospice, bringing her light and support into the lives of the people and families she serves by "teaching the art of living and dying well".

"Celebrations of Life" is what Rev. Pat is known best for. She owns WeddingsInSTL.com and assists couples in creating the perfect ceremony. Choices of officiates, customized wedding vows, location and preferred vendors can help make the wedding or event uniquely designed and effortlessly executed.

Connect Rev. Pat at: www.revpatpowers.net

Awake & Aware

By Rev. Pat Powers

I was floating in a sea of uncertainty, submersed in the undertow of chaos and victimization. Every area of my life was negative. My aging mother lived with my family and was ill—and needed more care than we could give. My friends were needy, dysfunctional and draining my life force. Our finances were just a reflection of the confusion and chaos in the other areas of life. I loved my husband and children—yet all of life felt overwhelming and felt out of my control. The God I knew as a child was absent.

Something had to change. A friend invited me to join her on a Sunday morning to learn about a different way of life that might offer a shift for me. Well, "I didn't go to church"—I had been there and done that. She explained that the motto of her community was "change your thinking and change your life". I had nothing to lose and everything to gain. So I went.

I discovered the God of my childhood was not the same Supreme Being spoken of at the Center for Spiritual Living. This was a personal Spirit, and the relationship opportunity was up to me to develop and utilize. No dogma—no rules—no limitations. I discovered a deep and profound Spiritual connection with a power greater than I remembered. God literally changed my life. I did change my thinking, I did change my choices and my language; and I changed my life.

Spiritual connection is different from religious connections. Spirituality is more universal and inclusive. It's my practice to capitalize the many names, qualities and attributes of God. My intention is to leave the subject of 'organized religion' completely out of this discussion and focus on 'spirituality'...the idea of having our own personal relationship and connection with the Spirit.

I had the opportunity to wake up to potential and possibility. Once **awake**, I was able to become **aware**. The reality of chaos and limitation in my life was a reflection of my words and my thinking. I began to **understand** the Universal Principles and how they are always working, even without my awareness. Recognize the negativity—and reframe it. I learned to **affirm** and declare a new life and a new way of being.

My path of Spiritual connection is available for anyone willing to become **awake** and **aware**—**understand** the belief systems that create our lives, **disassociate** with the negative and **affirm** and declare their desires. Awareness leads to understanding. Understanding leads to re-choosing (trading in the negative and accentuating the positive). The new choices are supported by affirmations and actions.

When we have a relationship with our Spiritual Nature (with our God Self, the God of our understanding, Spirit, the Christ Consciousness, Universal Energy, the Holy Spirit, Jesus, Buddha, Moses, Allah, Shiva or any name we call our Higher Power), we can learn to lead our lives from the guidance and wisdom of that which is greater than we are. We begin to understand we can be in deliberate creation and are manifesting our lives by the choices we make. Once we become clear about what we believe and who we are, we can begin to affirm our desires.

As we are "transformed by the renewing of our minds" (Romans 2:12), we know the "connection" is working. We know it has helped us, and we know our lives are better; and we are happier.

So what is Spiritual for you? I discovered my answer. The fun part is that your answer and my answer might be two different answers; and both of us are right – for us. Ernest Holmes, the founder of Religious Science, says:

> "God is not a person; God is a Presence personified in us. Spirituality is not a thing; it is the atmosphere of God's Presence, goodness, truth and beauty. Religion is life, a living." (*Science Of Mind*)

This idea of Divine Spirit "personified" in me opens me to the concept of Oneness. Once we have made the connection and made it consciously, we begin to learn and understand our personal Spiritual Nature. We understand our personal role in allowing our own Divinity to shine, of letting our "little light shine". Some of us even become willing to share our "big, bright, brilliant beam of radiant light shine" (lyrics of *Shine*, a song by Karen Drucker, www.KarenDrucker.com).

One path to sharing our light is to realize we are not the only ones who think in this way. As we connect with others of like mind, we find our out-of-the-box thinking is not so out of the box. "Cultural Creatives" are one in four. These are people seeking love, inspiration and fulfillment. We find, discover or build our communities and support each other.

When we connect with the One Power and Presence (by whatever name we call it), when we connect with our faith tradition (whatever it may be), we feel empowered.

You can connect with God when you are ill, when you are racked by physical ailments and begin feeling better, healthier and loved through affirmation and well being. Connect when you have struggle, and discover motivation and inspiration. Connect when you are sad or depressed, and discover joy and a positive life force.

Affirmative prayers are one way to connect with God. These are scientific, methodical prayers asking for our mind to accept the gifts God is always willing to give. We begin with **recognition**, recognizing God as All there is, the Source of All...Absolute. Next **unify** your own nature with the qualities of Spirit. Claim your desires in the first person, positive, present tense. The next step is called **realization**, when we state the essence of our request: "I am right now swimming in the Divine Flow of Good, of Compassion and Joy". This method includes **thanksgiving**, gratitude for all that is and all that is to come. Lastly is **release**. Releasing the outcome of our prayer and anticipating "this or something greater".

You can awaken to the way of spirit. It may have happened yesterday or twenty years ago, but now is the time to take action. What are your next steps now in deepening your understanding, expression and spiritual connection?

This may mean deepening and studying—bringing timeless principles and ancient wisdom squarely into this present time with dramatic relevance and rich implications. Having a Spiritual connection may mean you seek a community of people who think like you do. It may mean you read more. It may mean you connect with regular spiritual coaching. Your Spiritual Connection may bring you joy and happiness, even bliss.

> "My idea of true spirituality is that a man should live a perfectly normal life, entering into and enjoying all in life that is clean and good. He should place himself absolutely under the divine guidance. Other than this, he will seem just like other people, neither better nor worse…. You are spiritual in so far as you trust in the Spirit, at all times, in all places, under all conditions" (*Discover a Richer Life*).

Our Spiritual Connection allows us to take the message of modern day movies like *The Secret*, and *What the Bleep Do I Know* and apply the Law of Attraction to our everyday lives. Let us focus on what we want, let us keep the vision, and keep the high watch. Develop your own intention statement. Discover your life purpose. Create affirmations or positive declarations to support your desires. Make it a point to connect frequently.

First, 'Talk the Walk', then 'Walk the Talk', then 'Talk the Talk', then 'Walk the Walk'. These things are possible for you…and you will find your answers along the path.

In closing, I want to encourage you with the words of Irish poet, Oscar Wilde…"Be yourself, everyone else is already taken".

About the Author

Joe Craig, PhD, is a certified hypnotherapist and practiced holistic/spiritual healer. With his PhD from American Pacific University of Honolulu, Hawaii, and certification from the American Board of Hypnotherapy, he has helped many people overcome destructive patterns, both from a behavioral standpoint and through spiritual approaches. Reach him at: www.onprps.com or email: onprps.doc@gmail.com.

12-Step Programs –
The Programs of Paradox

By Joe Craig

As a person who has practiced in, and studied, 12-Step Programs for more than 25 years, I was asked to share insights I have gained. I have found that I learn best when I teach what I profess to believe. My experiences have shown me that by doing this, I gain an even more profound understanding (dare I say "greater wisdom"), while benefiting others as we talk about spirituality and its role in the 12-Step Recovery Programs.

The reader would benefit to realize that "The 12-Step Programs" are not self-help. Although many people initially look upon the 12-Steps as "Self-Help", this is one of the biggest misnomers we must face. The 12-Steps of Alcoholics Anonymous, originally scribed by Bill Wilson and edited by members of AA in 1939, are at the heart of many similar and complementary programs (i.e. Gamblers Anonymous, Narcotics Anonymous, Over-Eaters Anonymous, etc.). The 12-Steps are the essence of each spiritually-based program, yet any effective 12-Step Program is a paradox, contradictory to everything logic dictates. However, they (the 12 Steps) are an important part of the process for surrendering oneself over to one's own "Higher Power".

The definition "Self-Help" implies that I, on my own, am taking the steps to change my life; but nothing could be further from the truth. If I could change my life, once I realized that alcohol, gambling, cocaine or narcotics, etc. was destroying my relationships, my finances, my reputation and/or my life, I would simply take steps to avoid these activities or substances. Doing so would straighten out my life. For some people, such self-help methodologies of "natural recovery" seem to be effective. The 12-Step Programs are not needed by such people. The 12-Step Programs are clearly "Higher-Power-Help" or "God-Help".

Typically, a person comes to 12-Step Programs after having tried all the self-help programs he or she can find and falls short, as obsessions return stronger and stronger; and he or she returns to active participation in destructive behavior. In fact, such people report that they have no idea why they returned to the behavior they knew to be destroying themselves. This, we believe, is the definition of "insanity", as expressed in the Second Step of all the 12-Step Programs. They find that they do not have the ability to stay away from the destructive behavior by their own will power...that the ability must come from a Higher Power.

The Big Question is, "How does the individual connect with his or her Higher Power?" Spiritual leaders often teach there is only one problem that leads to all the problems of human kind and only one solution. The problem is Separation—separation from our fellows and separation from God. The solution is to smash the human ego, because it is the human ego which produces this separation. The 12-Steps are ideally suited to eliminate the blocks between person and person and between person and God.

I've heard it remarked that the 12-Steps give a person's conscious mind something to think about, while his or her Higher-Self removed all the blocks to conscious contact with God. This actually sets up a paradox (and it is important to remember that all great spiritual truths are paradoxical in nature). **On one hand, "Working the Steps" is not the solution that is sought; on the other hand, the solution can only be obtained through "Working the Steps".**

"Why did the addict, alcoholic or compulsive gambler work the steps?" They work the steps "to have a spiritual awakening or spiritual experience, as **THE result** of these steps".

The First Step defines the problem: admitting we are powerless, and our lives have become unmanageable. The Second Step defines the solution: a Power greater than us can restore us to sanity. In the Third Step, the person decides to seek the solution. The rest of the steps are the action steps so that the person might, first, have the solution appear in his or her life and, second, maintain that solution.

One troubling aspect about people who need a 12-Step Program is that, to him or her, the destructive behavior appears to be the solution to his or her life problems. Falsely grounded in this misperception, the person "...has no mental defense against the..." beginning of the next binge. Getting the person past this fact is what the First Step is all about. Remember, in the AA program, the First Step says, "We admitted we were powerless over alcohol; that our lives had become unmanageable".

The other 12-Step Programs have a similar First Step, related to the destructive behavior that is being addressed. When translated these first steps say, **"Our lives were not working when we**

were engaged in our destructive behaviors. At the same time, our lives were not working when we weren't engaged in our destructive behaviors." When such a statement describes a person's life, he or she has put his- or herself beyond human aid. So the power must come from beyond the individual or, even, from beyond individuals in the group. This leads to the Second Step.

"Came to believe that a Power Greater than ourselves could restore us to sanity." If my problem is just alcohol, the solution is eliminating alcohol from my life. If my problem is some behavior that is destroying my life, my solution is rigorously eliminating the destructive behavior. If, on the other hand, I continue to obsess about the behavior which I know is causing increasing negative consequences, and I come up with inconsequential excuses to participate in the behavior, I must gain the power to stop from outside of myself. **At the beginning, a new person can get some strength from the group; however, after a relatively short time, that strength must come from beyond human sources.**

It must be remembered that the "insanity" alluded to here is defined as, "Doing the same thing over and over again, expecting different results..." in the context of our destructive behavior. The insane thought is, "This time, despite all my past experiences to the contrary, the results will be different". The 12-Step Programs take the approach that the ultimate problem of the abnormal drinker, compulsive gambler, over-eater, drug user, etc. is in his or her head. Another thing to be noted about the Second Step is that there are no guarantees. It says that a higher power *could* restore us to sanity. Of course, this is contingent on following certain simple suggestions. So, the Second Step is theoretical only. It is simply done, not worked. Anyone who claims to be working the Second Step has either not read it or has not taken the First Step. Once the person takes the Second Step, the Third Step automatically follows.

Now, if a person thoroughly takes Step One, realizing at a deep level the hopelessness of his or her life as it is currently going, and acknowledges the theoretical concept that some higher power could restore him or her to sanity, then the Third Step follows logically, unless the person reads more into the step than is written. The Step says: "Made a decision to turn our will and our lives over to the care of God, as we understood Him."

There are those who have told me, "I am going to wait until I know what God's will for me is". This step says nothing about God's will. We are not instructed to ask for knowledge of God's will until the Eleventh Step, after the person has had his or her Higher Power relieve him or her of the "bondage of self". The Third Step basically says, "Since my life is dribbling down my sleeves, I don't have the power to make the changes necessary, and there is a Higher Power that could effect the necessary psychic change, I am deciding to get in touch with such a Power."

Perhaps it is in the hopelessness of our own situation that we find the greatest hope of all...the conscious contact with the God of our understanding. I have heard that another of the paradoxes of 12-Step Programs is that it is in being weak that we are made strong; and perhaps it is in being utterly helpless that we find the path of helpfulness to others.

God Bless you on your journey.

Seven Points of Impact

Point

2

Life Mission
& Purpose

About the Author

Linda F. Jacobsen is the founder and president of Global Vision Strategies, LLC. Her specialty is designing and facilitating customized solutions for global business, with emphasis on business development in China. Being multilingual, Linda has conducted over one thousand training sessions over the past fifteen years. Her expertise ranges from working with legal and cultural aspects of negotiating, to international human resources, diversity, global marketing, and training programs with both workplace and family focus. Her skills have evolved to include facilitating key global leadership meetings, world class keynote addresses, and diplomatic and trade representation around the world.

Linda's latest personal development challenge is pursuing her Ph.D. in International Higher Education at University of Missouri, St. Louis (UMSL). Her recent book, "Avoiding Burn-up on Re-entry", is designed with the needs of the relocating globalist in mind. Whether a soldier and family are trying to reunite or a worker and family are struggling through coming "home" again, this book will speak to those in need of advice. It's written by someone who's been there before and has learned even more from the thousands who have shared their stories with her. Visit www.GlobalVisionStrategies.com for additional information.

Thoughts on Living
an Extraordinary Life

By Linda Fraser Jacobsen

My life is an extraordinary one. I belong everywhere and nowhere. I have known this since I was a small girl. What I didn't know was how to take the curiosity, the joyful zeal, the intelligence and passion for life and synthesize these parts of me into something with focus that would help others. For that's what my whole life is about—how to make a difference in the lives of others. Knowing this single thing about me has made most days richer, fuller, more incredible. I have learned to take nothing for granted, how to live and give in the present, and how to see coincidences as anything but. Even the simplest of contacts, a single conversation, can transform into a path of choices that has outcomes with high value to others and high impact on how I feel about myself and my time on this earth. But more important is the question I ask now; how do *you* feel about your *own* life and its purpose?

No matter what you have chosen to do for a living or what you wish to transition to throughout your life, you have options as to *how* you will execute a choice most days of your life. Many of us fall into a passive pattern of ambivalence, feeling that others control our freedom, our choices and our outcomes. This is not the case. It is in how we *allow* ourselves to view our situation that everything becomes colored with our own perceptions. We are all products of the environments in which we were raised, siblings or solitude, hugs or smacks, the prejudices and passions, the love and the sadness, the fears and the flaws, the opportunities and the missed ones.

Are you ready to look beyond the overlay of your own perceptions, explore your deepest wishes, desires, hopes and dreams? If you don't make time to dream, to really listen to your heart's desire, you are merely going through the motions of daily life without *truly* living. Finding time to delve into your deepest desires, facing the obstructions honestly, and knowing where you really want to be, what you really want to be doing, I believe, is the most profound gift of intellect. It is the gift of living in the true present through self-knowledge and constant self-assessment.

Knowing that I was a citizen of the world was far different from being able to live out that knowledge. I had to find a way to align my passions and intentions with real experiences and training to bring purpose and value to the present. Probably the greatest step I had to take was to let go of the past. Throwing away the old lens of perceptions of my past gave me the chance to see more clearly what it was I most wanted for myself, what I already had, and how I defined happiness. What I learned is that most of us aren't aware that we let others define us and then wonder why we are unhappy or dissatisfied in some ways.

We fall into this trap easily when we don't take time to consider our own needs and desires, some of which can be deeply buried or suppressed under patterns of the present and the past. Instead, we let everything going on around us on the outside define who we are and what we do. The inner self needs to be explored, discovered, defined and then expressed through solid alignment with the outer environment, through how we choose to act. Only each of us on an individual journey can decide what that inner self knows and craves and then seek the outer experiences, people and opportunities to bring the two into alignment. This process of aligning inner spiritual needs with outer actions and choices is how I would explain my own pathway to a purposeful life.

There is nothing selfish in exploring our own deeply buried hopes, dreams or desires. It is my belief that, in making time for self-assessment and deep exploration, we are living to our most profound depth in the true present and acknowledging the gift we have been given. The world changes around us every moment, every breath. If we are not looking around at all the possibilities, if we are not counting ourselves in as part of the formula for positive growth and change at any given moment, we are wasting an opening to have an equally profound impact on the world around us and the people sharing the journey.

Sit still in a place you do your best thinking. Close your eyes and breathe, and listen to your own breathing. Feel your chest rise, your ribcage expand, your nostrils tighten; exhale and know you are alive and what a gift exists in this moment. What will you do with all this amazing potential? Keep breathing, feeling the breath course in and out of your miraculous body. Know the magic of the next breath and the next. The gift of the present is here, with you, and only you can understand what you need to do with the time you have been given. Only you can define it.

During one of my "sit still and breathe" sessions, I let my mind wander. It came to me (probably from having heard something on one of the science documentaries I love to watch on the Discovery Science channel) that the molecules of air we breathe have been around since the dawn of time. I began to imagine what part per million I might be breathing in, right then, that someone I admired in world history had also breathed in and out. I felt immediately connected in time and space with some of the most incredible people. I felt their presence all around me, thanked them for their contributions, and knew that they had walked the earth just as I was able to now. What a gift it was to be alive in this time and place, to have learned what they shared, and now have the addition of technology exponentially moving people into a new era of thinking, working, and developing. How could I make the most of my time, here and now?

While in India a few years back, where I'd been invited to address a convention of women entrepreneurs from all over south Asia, I met a man who grabbed my hands and looked at my palms very closely. He did not speak English, and I did not speak Hindi; but we connected all the same. The gentle, intent man smiled into my eyes and kept hold of my hands, speaking with clear, yet calm, excitement to the people around us. I had never before been approached in this fashion, but my curiosity was on high alert, wondering at the meaning of this interaction. Another young man came up to interpret for us, and what he shared startled me; and I think of it to this day. The man reading my palms said I had an extraordinary marking near my pinkie, something he'd only seen once before in his life, in Mahatma Gandhi. Think of it. You may choose to shrug it off as foolishness or something mysterious beyond our understanding or you may think of it as I did...a call to reach for my highest self, to do the greatest possible good for others while I am walking the earth. I choose to keep his words close to me always, to remind me that each of us has the potential to do all the good of Gandhi and many more like him who came before and will come after. The choice is yours, every day, every moment. But you must first take time to know your innermost desires. Sit still and breathe.

About the Author

Sue Cotta is an eclectic mix of passions and experiences. As a compassionate person, who happens to be a physical therapist, she helps people listen to their 'inner wisdom' with a combination of her hands-on work and unconditional presence.

As co-owner of the St. Louis and St. Charles County Women's Journals, Sue is tireless in her pursuit of newspaper excellence and believes firmly in inspiring and informing readers. She splits her time between visiting St. Louis, MO and living in Swansea, MA. You may reach her through the Women's Journals at susan@Womens-Journals.com.

Sue has also written the children's book, *I Can Show You I Care: Compassionate Touch for Children*, which is a book about how children (and adults) can change the world through touch. You may reach Sue or order an autographed copy of her children's book or this book through her website www.SueCotta.com.

Live Your Passion —
Live Your Purpose

By Sue Cotta

Living your life mission or purpose may seem like a daunting or unattainable possibility. For many, living their life mission becomes apparent only after they've lived life and can reflect upon their experiences. For others, it seems to be something they just know. I fall into the latter camp, having always known, on some level, the bigger picture of my life's mission was to make a difference in the lives of others and serve the world in some way.

I've also always known that the world could not be a perfect place without each of us fulfilling our own special spot in it. It's up to each of us to find our specialness and live it—no matter how small or large it is.

My life is an amazing journey full of fun, surprises, sorrow and joy through all of my ventures. Along the way, I've learned some valuable lessons—most of all, to stay true to myself.

I grew up in a supportive environment with two loving parents who provided me with the freedom to explore many different options in life. I've always been a hard, conscientious worker, starting at an early age helping my dad. Once I was old enough to get a "real" job waitressing, it enabled me to put myself through undergraduate and graduate school. While pursuing a physical education degree, I coached a girls' little league softball team.

I loved the small, motivated group of girls that I coached, but realized that teaching the large classes often seen in public schools was not my path.

So, after graduating, I immediately went into physical therapy. While in PT school, I worked part-time for group homes which housed people with various disabilities, helping them to live on their own. After achieving my PT degree, I began working as a physical therapist in various hospital settings. I quickly added a small, private PT practice to this endeavor, as I craved the independence of my own practice. I've also dabbled in real estate and had an environmental consulting business for over five years.

I eventually left the hospital setting and now have my own private PT practice, incorporating traditional PT, as well as non-traditional modalities which address the physical, mental, emotional and spiritual aspects of people (becoming an ordained minister in 1999). My passion for teaching had also found its place, teaching CranioSacral Therapy (CST) to motivated adults.

The biggest lesson I learned from these varied experiences is that life lessons are learned no matter what you're doing at the time. Sometimes we learn that our decisions just aren't quite right for us, and we change course to be closer to our truth. I still have my PT practice, and I still enjoy pursuing new opportunities.

As an example, in 2004, my sister, Kristin, and I decided to embark upon a joint venture. Together we purchased a marketing plan for the Women's Journals, a newspaper dedicated to informing and inspiring its readership. The decision was easy;

I love working with my sister who has the same mission as I do. We felt the Women's Journals would provide a forum to help women and do it en masse instead of one at a time.

The years since have been an adventure for us. We've had to learn the newspaper business and create an organization from the ground up. We've experienced many late nights and angst over rising costs; but neither of us would trade what we've learned or the people we've met along the way for anything.

In early 2010, we decided to undertake a major challenge. We wanted to make a bigger impact, not only in the St. Louis area, but in the world. So, the "Make It Happen Event" was born. Our vision, which seemed to be ever-changing, was to create not just an event with booths and speakers, but an experience that could truly impact the individual, the community and the world.

It was a huge project. I took on the bulk of the responsibilities and coordination for its development. I did it willingly and happily, at least in the beginning. I was so energized and consumed by the amount of effort needed to create something so special, impactful and life-changing, that it almost blinded me to how it was affecting me.

My first awareness came when I realized I was feeling as if I had to make the "Make It Happen Event" happen. The ease and flow I had started with was gone. Part of me thought I could 'muscle' through it. The other, growing part knew that the Event was becoming too difficult; and there were more "red flags" popping up. I began to think I might actually get sick if I continued.

But the wheels were turning, the venue was booked, sponsorships had been sold; how could I possibly back away now? When doubts began seeping into my consciousness, and my body began to register its unhappiness by keeping me up at night (preventing me from getting to my "quiet thinking space"), I started to think that this great idea was not such a great idea at this particular time in my life.

So I looked objectively at the situation and weighed all the advice from others. After many hours spent in contemplation, despite that it meant disappointing people who had volunteered to help, I cancelled the event, admitting what I wanted wasn't right for me now; and muscling through it wasn't possible. I knew I could survive the shock, surprise and possible hurt feelings that might surface if I stopped the Make It Happen Event. I knew we'd be refunding money and potentially losing some, too. However, I was smart enough to realize that if I had to 'push' upstream to create something, I was no longer being true to myself.

What I'm hoping you'll take away from this story is that sometimes, to get where you want to go, you may have to go backwards, take a detour or simply walk away. It's okay to not have everything figured out; but the one thing you must not do is stay stuck in inaction—especially if you have to back away from something you really want.

I love the Robert Schuller quote, "What would you do, if you knew you could not fail?" We place so much negative emphasis on failing; we never stop to consider that from failure comes learning and experience. If we think of failure in this context, then isn't Failure simply Success disguised as a learning opportunity?

Finding an outlet for our life's mission may take many forms. We may travel down a variety of paths, hoping that this one will be the right one. I suggest that every path is the right path, for going down each means we learn, grow and expand our thinking. Each one brings us that much closer to the place where our life's mission and its most beautiful expression finally meet. It's at that juncture when all that's come before suddenly makes perfect sense.

> "Often the difference between a successful person and a failure is not one has better abilities or ideas, but the courage that one has to bet on one's ideas, to take a calculated risk – and to act."
>
> Andre Malraux

About the Author

 As a professional speaker, business promoter, radio show host and emcee, Kelley Lamm uses humor, laughter, hope, love and compassion to encourage others to embrace life's challenges. She believes these are the essential ingredients to inspire us to make life-affirming choices and take positive actions to live life to the fullest. Her heartfelt desire is to help create a world that is "Deliciously Alive" by encouraging people to explore, ignite and indulge in every sweet opportunity life has to offer...regardless of the outward appearance of situations or circumstances.

Kelley has been told that she has a personality full of sugar and spice...something to be proud of when we consider the life circumstances and challenges she has overcome. Although no stranger to adversity, she used these experiences to develop a deep appreciation for all the bittersweet chocolate flavors of life. There was gratitude for the times of sweet abundant bounty and acceptance for the harsh contrast of bitter personal struggles. Kelley discovered, as we all must, that all these moments produce the luscious flavors of life.

In the Midwest you may connect with Kelley on WESTPLEX Radio 100.7 FM with the "Deliciously Alive" show. Regionally you can connect with Kelley on the "Be Deliciously Alive" tour or private bookings may be arranged through the KelleLamm.com web site.

BitterSweet

By Kelley Lamm

Life is BitterSweet...Like chocolate, it's a mixture of sweet and bitter, light and dark, pleasure and pain.

Chocolate! CHOC-O-LAT...Now that's a heavenly word that conjures up describable memories of sensual moments, rich fantasies, deep dark secrets, and luxurious pleasures. Is there a man, woman or child who has not lusted after it, dreamed of it or found themselves devouring it?

BitterSweet moments begin the day we are born, and each of those moments is filled with challenges and an incredible desire to survive. The journey through life can be delightfully sweet, filled with the meltingly lovely taste of milk chocolate or completely bitter, like raw cacao...unbearable to swallow... challenging us to turn the bitter into sweet. Challenges come our way and they change our lives forever. Sometimes we're not able to clearly see our choices through the darkness of the long night, and we're paralyzed. We curl into a tiny little ball unable to move, not speaking for fear of what we might say, fighting back that primal scream erupting from our insides. We can't open our eyes for fear of what we will see...and we are unable to listen for fear of what we might hear.

My life has been filled with the bitter and the sweet. The sweetness comes from my two beautiful daughters, Karly and Kasey. But then there were the hard times—times when it seemed the only chocolate I had to choose from was dark and bitter. But I'm still standing...I'm still alive...and I'm still moving forward. How...did...that...happen?

I've asked myself a thousand times how I survived when the doctors told me I had cancer. How did I bear it when I was faced with a life-threatening infection? Why didn't I give up when I miscarried? How did I survive a devastating divorce, the loss of a loved one? I built a business from the ground up and then lost it to an economy gone suddenly sour. How did I endure? Where did the answer come from when my little girl asked me, "Mommy, will we have to live in our car?" The challenges swirled around me and engulfed me in a rage of pain and fear. How did I survive that bittersweet journey?

I survived because I recognized my challenges, explored my future and created my mission...to help myself and others "Be Deliciously Alive". I had faith in my choices and ignited them with positive intentions. Filled with courage, I was determined to finish my past, embrace change and deliciously indulge in new opportunities that would bring life-changing directions for me.

I survived because of the desire to make a difference in the lives of others, the passion to persevere and the unconditional love shared with my two beautiful daughters.

Kasey, now a young adult, is stunning and her passion is to make people beautiful. She never forgets a funny movie line and is great at cracking jokes. She also helps me promote our children's book series.

Karly, who is at the threshold of her teenage years, is brilliantly creative at writing poetry and magical melodies. She is already researching and hopes to find a cure for cancer.

One day, after many bitter moments...during the time when I was fighting for my very life...young Karly said to me, "Momma, have faith". Then she wrote these unforgettable words:

> *"You can't see air, but you still breathe it.*
> *You can't hear God, but you believe it.*
> *Momma, faith is here; yes, it's nice and clear.*
> *Clear your mind; let Him take you that way;*
> *look forward, not back.*
> *God gave two eyes to look forward, so forget the past,*
> *Cherish the moments and grasp what lasts.*
> *Receive your loving; do good, not bad.*
> *Then you wait and see, faith comes around*
> *and then you will receive.*
> *Momma, have faith. Momma, I love you."*

I've learned life is a canvas waiting for us to paint our beautiful journey of memories—memories that create our portrait. Living can be so beautiful if we just let it paint itself and quit forcing the brush strokes. I've learned to have faith in life...focusing on my future and finishing my past...for the dark night concludes and the new dawn breaks forth with all its blessed possibilities.

The bittersweet lessons of my life encouraged me to stretch and catch a glimpse of my beautiful surroundings, memories that made me smile, and remember all the reasons I'm alive. I learned to be gentle and kind...to be brilliant and bright...to be patient and polite. Most of all, I have learned to guide my life in the direction I want it to go.

So paint your path where you want to go, make a splash and leave a mark. Don't be afraid to make mistakes, take a chance at life. Life is filled with really big challenges; but those challenges create amazing choices, and those choices can change the direction of your life. The ability to embrace change, accept what is next and live each day as if it were your last is the "BitterSweet" lesson.

Take the time to help one person at a time see the importance of a meaningful smile, warm laughter and a helping heart. Don't fail to appreciate the beauty around you. Make life simple, make dreams come true, and make memories last forever.

Let Laughter Erupt. Let Love Shine. Let go of the past and step into a pallet of color. Explore, ignite and indulge in sweet opportunities...then take life-changing action to become deliciously alive! Cavette Roberts, a famous motivational speaker, once said, "If you don't think everyday is a great day, just try missing one."

Our journey is BitterSweet, a mixture of both pleasure and pain. Take those days of challenges and work your way through them the best you can. Find faith. Define hope. Deify the odds. Live deliciously, filled to the brim with meaningful purpose, every day you are given. For in the end, our life is a canvass rich with new beginnings, bright colors, incredible challenges, amazing choices and positive changes...created one brush stroke at a time. We are all a magnificent work of art in progress. Some day each of us will have a canvas beautifully painted, filled with memories, finished and framed, but never forgotten.

Written by Kelley Leamm   Illustrated by Susie Angelo

Kocoa and the Chocolate Fairy – A Children's book series

As the author of the "Kocoa and the Chocolate Fairy", children's book series, Kelley offers positive stories of inspiration for kids who wish to have amazing adventures, beautiful dreams and magical moments. If you want your children or grandchildren to be nurtured with positive messages, books are available for purchase through the web site: www. KocoaandtheChocolateFairy.com.

About the Author

Kathy Wasserman is an avid philanthropic and community volunteer. She lives in St. Louis, Missouri, where she has been a successful event planner and entrepreneur. She shares her zest for living and her sincere love of people in all of her pursuits, both personally and professionally. In addition to the various charities she supports, Kathy currently serves as an independent project manager, fundraiser and event planner for diverse endeavors, such as The Atai Orphanage, Zonta International, Crystal City Underground Cave, the Gambling Balance Organization and The Seven Points of Impact Project. Her annual "Friends of Kids with Cancer" Halloween Party is the cornerstone of the autumn philanthropy calendar in St. Charles County, Missouri.

Working closely with a wide range of volunteers, patrons, philanthropists and corporate or community sponsors, Kathy works tirelessly to maximize the impact of organizations from established charities to grassroots initiatives and organizations.

If you also seek the positive treasures and potential that the future holds, visit Kathy's personal website for more information about the current projects and initiatives in which she is enthusiastically involved. www.kathywasserman.com

To schedule or attend a 7 Points of Impact event in your area, please visit: www.7PointsOfImpact.com.

Discovering Possibilities

Looking for the Treasures of Life

By Kathy Wasserman

I am a treasure hunter at heart. I love to walk along the beach, deliberately guiding my metal detector across the path...basking in joyous anticipation of that once-in-a-lifetime find. Will it be a diamond tennis bracelet, a gold ring or a precious antique coin? Nuts, bolts, bottle caps, pennies and the sparkle of the sand are more likely to be the find of the day; but still I search. Not knowing what may be next sustains the adventurous heart.

Reflecting on this spirit of adventure, I realize that when I walk on the beach, it is not the waiting or anticipation that captivates me. Instead, my true enjoyment comes from contemplating the possibilities and actively taking each step towards the future. In this moment, each successive step offers boundless potential and surprise; it is this experience that is the treasure. Waiting, by its very nature, delivers nothing. Yet, seeking out what destiny may lay beneath the sand uncovers the sparkle of this simple joy attainable to all. When we cherish each moment as an individual coin in the treasure chest of life, each circumstance, situation, event and person becomes infinitely more exciting and valuable. With this spirit, I am inspired to discover and continue exploring.

Our exploration does not need to be limited to a solitary pursuit on the beach. By sharing life with our family and friends every day, we recognize the relationships that define our heritage, our legacy, our traditions and our world. These precious relationships thrive when exposed to the sun; yet they are the very relationships that we often take for granted, leaving them buried for special occasions or holiday gatherings. All too frequently people forget to find joyful moments so close at hand. How often do we let the daily grind and pressures of life rob us of these treasures? Unless we are mindful, these opportunities for closeness can slip away underneath the masking sand of our inconsequential worries and everyday stresses. When we choose to be mindful of our everyday relationships and rejoice in these treasures, the energy we discover brings more good, more love, more joy and better health. This is the true alchemy of wealth.

Seeking wealth is both a noble and popular pursuit. The true characterization of this, however, depends on how one defines wealth. For some, it is a simple balance sheet; others seek a more intangible energy. I believe that each representation has merit, but my spirit seeks the nuance of the discovery itself. Combining an appreciation for the treasures of the unknown with a celebration of each daily encounter shapes my ambition and life. When I meet a new person or learn more about those with whom I am already associated, I recognize that our paths have crossed for a reason. Whether it is for a fleeting moment at a party, an introduction through friends or even sharing a travel delay in an airport, each occasion provides another opportunity to discover the exhilarating potential in these otherwise chance meetings. Through conversation, enthusiasm and openness, we uncover yet another treasure. It may not be material riches, but making a new friend or deepening an existing friendship will, indeed, leave you feeling the sand between your toes.

Leaving the beach behind and being prepared for adventure wherever you may go can be intimidating. There is uncertainty in showing enthusiastic openness, and it can often uncover feelings of vulnerability. Instead of focusing on the risk of a situation, I take the steps to contemplate the potential. Ask yourself, "What if...?" But just as sure as you ask yourself this question, embrace the spirit of discovery and answer any doubt with the qualification "up until now". My close friend, Linda Fitzgerald, shared this philosophy with me from her writings. The adage "until now" enables one to shift intentions towards greater potential, acknowledging a reflection on the past, yet leaving aside any harsh evaluation in favor of excitement about the future. Until now, you may not have answered your "what if" with an affirmation. Until now, you may not have valued simple pleasures, everyday happiness or the love and laughter around you. Until now, you may not have readily unearthed the treasures so apparently in front of you. Until Now!

From recognizing the joy that is present in your daily life, you must continue to shape your life with positivity. In seeking treasure on the beach, I am making a decision to spend time both relaxing and contemplating the possibilities. Just as one would take another step in the sand, you must also ask yourself, "What will I do to make a positive impact?" It may simply be sharing a smile or kind word. In discovering the new, we are blessed with the responsibilities of sharing joy.

I am especially fond of children and believe they, themselves, embody the potential for good; therefore, I ask myself, "Can I be the catalyst for joy in a child's life? Can I create a positive ripple in my world?" My answer is, undoubtedly, "Yes". I am no saint, no billionaire philanthropist; and I need not be one to make an impact. It simply takes answering the next question: "When will I make this positive impact?" To this question, the answer of a truly committed adventurer is…"starting now".

In contrast to "until now", the phrase "starting now" is encouragement that we ourselves determine the future. We, ourselves, through belief and action, place that next treasure in our own paths. Viewing our lives through the spirit of "starting now" reminds you that, with every decision you face, there is a positive choice. Just as with every interaction with a friend, family or total stranger, kindness and enthusiasm can lead to that next great ripple. Washing the sand off of buried treasure is, therefore, only a matter of time.

Even a modest life can be full of meaning, offering a lasting legacy of love and joy. In living a positive life, you will most quickly and effectively make your way towards greatness through generous gestures. It is not hard to enjoy the adventure, if we are self-aware. Just as I continue my walk along the waterfront with untold riches ahead of my magnetic wand, I encourage each of you to shape your own path with a similar, contemplative divining rod, asking those important "what if" questions. When faced with a question such as this, be prepared to confidently recognize the gravitas of "until now", a truly cleansing and empowering concept; and then happily usher in that next step towards a more positive and joyful future with a simple "starting now" phrase.

Kathy can show you how to step forward towards "Discovering Possibilities" and finding the treasures in your life. She works closely with the *7 Points Authors* to collaborate events throughout the country. To schedule a *7 Points of Impact* event in your area or to attend a workshop or keynote by these transformational coaches, please visit: www.7PointsOfImpact.com.

About the Author

Aprille Trupiano, *International Coach, Speaker, Author,* is described by clients as being bold, completely straight, high energy, vivacious and dedicated. Her talent for being creative, engaging people in actions that will fulfill their goals, and encouraging others to think outside the ordinary redefines how they see themselves. Her practical mix of how-to and high dose of inspiration leaves people empowered and effective. Her proven systems catapult clients to the miraculous in their lives and the extraordinary in their businesses, where all their purest desires and their most intense passions are reborn. Aprille's clients become fully engaged in their lives and their inevitable success surfaces so they're fully realized, as they are born to be, and living their most passionate lives!

Aprille first became an entrepreneur at the age of 20 and has been creating, building, and expanding businesses ever since. Having built companies from the ground up to six and seven figures, Aprille has developed systems and processes that she shares with her private coaching clients and exclusive Mastermind groups so they can effortlessly do the same thing. She coaches in the US and Italy.

Visit Aprille's website: www.AprilleTrupiano.com for her complimentary eCourse, "5 Mistakes Women Make from the Boardroom to the Bedroom".

Living a Regret-Free Life

by April Trupiano

It was September, 2000, and I was standing in a beautiful studio space with my realtor in Milan, Italy. I was finally stepping into my lifelong dream of owning my own fashion design business in the fashion capitol of the world. We were reviewing the rental contract when I got the call that altered my life forever.

My sister was on the line explaining they'd discovered my mother's partner was stealing from her. They'd gotten rid of him, and they needed someone to take over the business. I hung up, told the realtor "no thank you", then called my "angel investor" and told him things would be on hold for six months. I went back to my tiny flat, bought the first ticket to the States, packed a small roll-on bag and headed home to fix things on behalf of my family. October, 2010, marks my 10th year back in the United States.

People still ask me if I will ever return to fashion design, if I'll ever move back to Italy. They more often ask me if I regret my decision.

"You should have followed your dreams", they say.
"You would have been so fabulous at it", they tell me.
"You could have done it all", they add.
 I answer them, "I DID do it all."

Because the truth is, I did EXACTLY what was important to me. The moment I heard my sister's voice, the choice for me was simple, easy, a no brainer. Make sure my family is okay. In that moment, nothing else meant more. I didn't know it then, but I was doing precisely what I teach my entrepreneurs to do to ensure they thrive in their businesses and love their lives...live and work passionately.

Do I ever ask myself "what if"? Sure, for about 30 seconds; and then I move on, because on the other side of that "what if" is the "What if I HADN'T come home?" Where would my family be now? How would I feel knowing I'd pursued my dreams and yet let my family fail? At the time, my mother's business supported my entire family with everyone still living at home and one brother away at college. I wouldn't have pursued my fashion design business with the same fervor, constantly worrying about them. I surely wouldn't have enjoyed any sweetness in my successes knowing they came at the cost of my family's well being.

Let's put this into perspective as it relates to you. You say you know what you want...yet years go by and you still don't have the life you described or once imagined. You think you didn't make enough money to "have it all" or you didn't do it "right". You made poor choices or worse yet, you had to "sacrifice", so those things never came to fruition.

I say none of that is true. In fact, I say you have EXACTLY the life you chose.

I can say this because I have lived it myself—and my life has "turned out" fabulously (albeit differently) just as, I'm certain, has yours. Nonetheless, if you're not clear, it still leaves that tugging feeling at your heartstrings...it still has you sitting at the stoplight wondering how you got "here"...it still wakes you up at 3 a.m. asking yourself where your childlike passion went and how it got "like this".

The answer is simple. Somewhere along the way, you confused your goals with your values. You then began to pursue the goals without seeing if they actually aligned with your values. You see, values form our character and define us. They shape who we are and make us unique and memorable...distinct in the world. Values give our life meaning, purpose and direction. They determine our life choices, guide our behaviors and direct our lives. Our values make up who we are at the core of our beings. Goals, while they have merit, are objectives or milestones— things we want to accomplish, achieve or obtain. Huge difference! Reaching goals may satisfy us momentarily, but values fulfill the expression of who we are!

Ultimately, you'll always make the choices in life that fulfill your values. Can you see that, if decades pass and you wonder why you never had that lake house with the boat you dreamed of, but you've raised your family, put them through college, and taken care of your aging parents, you've actually done EXACTLY what your heart intended? You may feel like you "sacrificed" when, truthfully, you followed what really was most important to you! I'll bet if we sat down for a cup of coffee, I'd know instantly your family is more important to you than anything else. Now, you might still want that lake house and boat; and I say GO FOR IT if you've already realized everything else in life that takes priority for you. You've earned it, and perhaps now you could use that as a place to share beautiful moments with your grown family.

When you look at it this way, can you see that life is devoid of regrets? You can begin to appreciate the gifts you've had in your life and start planning the ones you're still dreaming of starting today!

When working with my entrepreneurial clients, I take them through a specific process so they can look closely at their lives and businesses and outline a Value Statement. Once they have a Value Statement, everything they do in life and business can be measured by that.

Roy Disney said, **"When your values are clear to you, making decisions becomes easier."** I couldn't agree more, which is why in my step-by-step program, "Successful, Sassy, Savvy You", this is where we begin the journey. Any decision you need to make in your life or your business will be simple to make, without the hesitation and second guessing. When you have such clarity, I promise you'll know when things feel "off"; and you'll see that there's a direct correlation between this feeling and an area of your values that needs truing up.

Let me give you an example. My personal Value Statement is:

Living a Life of Joy, Passion, Play.
Celebrating Family. Being a Contribution.
All this surrounded by Beauty.

I know that anytime I'm cranky and irritable, perhaps feeling out of sorts or unproductive in my office, one of these things is OFF! I do a quick "check in". At times, I've noticed that my office is feeling droopy and needs some fresh flowers or a new candle scent to beautify my environment. Other times, I realize I'm being just too darn serious about work and other issues, so I grab the bottle of bubbles that sits on my desk and blow away or get up and dance (yes, I said dance!). Sometimes I've been working too much, and I need more family in my life. Even though we hold the "Trupiano

Sunday Dinner" as a ritual family gathering, I might need more one-on-one time with my mother (my most favorite person in the Universe), so I call and make a date with her.

What can you do to true up your life and blow the lid off your business?

Let me leave you with these four simple steps:

1. Clarify your VALUES
   – Set your goals according to these values
2. Be certain you're living inside of your VALUES
   – Examine all areas of your life – personal, business, spiritual
3. Make only promises that align with YOUR values
   – Don't follow someone else's values if they conflict with yours
4. Avoid the "what if" game unless you're going to look at both sides
   – For each "what if I had" there is a "what if I hadn't" to consider

To Your Most Passionate Life!

About the Author

Steve O'Rourke (StephenRORourke.com) is an independent consultant who advocates for efficiency and sustainability through the intelligent use of energy and information. He promotes renewable energy and, in the process, educates prospects about the importance of energy efficiency and conservation. You can find more of his writings on his blog—IntelEfficient.com.

Steve has been married to his wife Maria (MariaRodgersORourke.com) for more than 15 years. Maria supports the family initiatives while still working as a popular and accomplished speaker, author, columnist and teacher. She helps people find deeper meaning in life with her spiritual insights and inspiring stories.

Together they have two children and are a family committed to a "green" lifestyle.

Global Guardian

By Stephen R. O'Rourke

I happened to be traveling on business the day after St. Patrick's Day, and I came across the perfect addition to my limited Irish attire. The Kelly-green baseball cap had the words "THINK GREEN" embroidered on the front, with the "I" in "THINK" serving as the trunk of a white oak tree. Now it must be known that, in addition to the pride of my Irish heritage, green has always been my favorite color, I love plants and nature, and the beautiful emerald is my birthstone. So it all fits together quite well.

I happened to be wearing this hat when I walked into a local restaurant. The young man who took my order recognized me as a regular customer and offered his unapologetic protest. "I'll think green when it's convenient", he said smiling...and not the least bit ashamed of what he'd just said. We had a brief, but friendly, dialog rather than a debate; but it left me wondering about how to appeal to his perspective.

The truth is I haven't always acted "green". I certainly didn't drive conservatively in my younger years or really even consider the notion of "sustainability". My first introduction to the concept was in college, when I took a Human Ecology course in 1980. This was the product of a growing awareness of environmental issues that, unfortunately, seemed to sizzle out after the initial progress made in the 1970s. The course content focused primarily on the effect of population growth on the finite natural resources of our planet. The facts I learned were alarming, and yet I comfortably resumed my lifestyle of entitlement when the semester ended.

In the 90s, my somewhat conservative, but independent, political ideology blossomed into a more progressive line of thinking. The boundaries between science and spirituality began to blur, and I began to develop a greater appreciation for the benefits of living in harmony with the Earth. I remember being graciously challenged by a neighbor about using toxic chemicals on my lawn and discovered the more organic alternatives available. This was an awakening experience as I began to consider that we all live "downstream". I began to look more closely at the labels on the foods I bought and grew increasingly skeptical about the truth of what I'd been lead to believe all my life by our corporate-owned media.

It became increasingly clear to me that energy was an essential issue that we needed to address on the planet. The growing scarcity and political insecurity around oil, coupled with the increasing concern about climate change, became driving forces behind the development of cleaner forms of energy. I learned that three US states (Texas, Kansas and North Dakota) had enough wind energy to power the entire country's electricity needs, though it would require significant investments in a deteriorating power distribution system. Yet the promise of renewable energy became a personal passion.

I also learned that more solar energy falls on the earth in a single *hour* than what is used by the entire global population in a *year*. Germany, which is somewhere between New Mexico and Montana in geographic size, led the world in installed solar power capacity until recently, when the US finally surpassed them. While Germany is endowed with the solar resource equivalent to that of Alaska, they have embraced the clean, renewable energy of the sun in a big way. While we continue to bicker about the aesthetic appeal of solar panels, Germans have found them completely compatible with buildings much older than our country.

My involvement in the renewable energy industry led me to discover the concept of sustainability. While Americans represent only five percent of the world's population, we consume 25% of the planet's resources. Our financial prosperity relies on materialism and economic growth; and as we outsource jobs to China and India, we look to those markets with great promise as their population adopts the western lifestyle of conspicuous consumption. When you do the projections, they are daunting. Mother Earth simply isn't fit to accommodate our lifestyle across the globe. In spite of my growing frugality, we would need three or four planets to sustain the world's population if everyone lived like me.

While energy is a fundamental resource that has ripple effects across our economy and environment, water is even more fundamental. Our planet is 70% water, but only two percent of that is fresh water, with the bulk of that tiny fraction in the form of ice. As that ice melts evermore quickly into the ocean as a result of climate change, our sea levels rise, threatening our coastal cities. However, global warming is also melting our ice-capped mountains, which serve as nature's storage device to supply water to arid areas during their dry season. The fundamental requirement for water will likely create increasing competition for scarce supplies, causing suffering at a minimum and potentially war as tensions escalate across borders.

I have come to understand that true health and happiness on our planet can only result from both environmental and social justice. We must not only live in harmony with the earth, but in harmony with each other in order to fully realize a sustainable world. Can economic growth and sustainability coexist? Can we continue to increase our food production to feed an ever-increasing number of people and livestock? Must we make choices to foster net-zero population growth or wait for a massive epidemic or widespread famine to bring things into balance?

It's going to take more than recycling trash and driving a hybrid to bring about true balance in the world. We can only achieve net-zero energy by combining renewable energy with *efficiency* and *conservation*. We need to begin to embrace a "cradle-to-cradle" approach to manufacturing, where *all* components of a manufactured product are recycled. This will require a significant shift in the design process—designing the product for de-manufacturing. For example, if electronics manufacturers were responsible for all of their waste, they would find better ways to build the products so that all of the materials could be reused in some way.

Another concept with incredible promise is bio-mimicry, where we observe, embrace and harness the miracles of nature. We've been doing this in a variety of ways since the beginning of time, and yet there is so much more potential to study how nature works. A classic example of this is the ever- present Velcro, which was modeled after the maddening cockleburs we've all picked off our clothing after a hike through the woods. Nature is full of ingenious ideas that, if we would simply look closely enough, could offer tremendous potential. Of course, we also need to exercise prudence and caution, particularly with genetic engineering.

In spite of the near unanimous agreement in the scientific community, there remain stalwart factions in our culture who continue to deny the truth about climate change, likely because this "inconvenient truth" threatens our comfortable lifestyle. The real truth is the earth will heal itself one way or another. We just might not like how things turn out if we don't change our ways.

Thankfully, there is a growing awareness of the need to "think green"; and as more people embrace this way of thinking, it's becoming more popular, affordable and convenient. With this, perhaps my young friend behind the restaurant counter will soon change his thinking and help change the planet. I encourage you to become part of this growing group of Global Guardians. As Gandhi said, "Be the change you wish to see in the world."

About the Author

 Patrice Billings retired in 2009 as a Chief Pilot after serving 28 years with the St Louis County Police Department. She knows a little something about beginning her dream with a destination in mind! Patrice took her love of aviation into a dream job as the first female police officer in the United States to become a helicopter pilot for a law enforcement agency in 1984.

Patrice now speaks to groups of all sizes and shares stories of survival, overcoming obstacles, and re-inventing oneself. Her transformational model called "Begin with a Destination in Mind" brings a blend of proven success principles to individuals and to the workplace.

Patrice is currently working on her first fiction novel to be published in 2011. Please visit: www.PatriceBillings.com

Begin With A Destination In Mind

By Patrice Billings

As a police helicopter pilot patrolling the skies above a large metropolitan area, I always began my flight with several factors in mind. Chief among those factors was a pre-determined destination or a **"Definite Major Purpose" (DMP)**. I set my intention *before* I took off as to where I ultimately wanted to land. To put it simply, I prepared a **flight plan** before I departed. I also employed a series of practical actions, or **navigational tools**, that helped ensure a successful flight.

Does that mean I never had course corrections to contend with? Quite the contrary! I learned to instinctively adapt to all of the variables of an airborne law enforcement mission. This included relying on my skills and training, accepting (even relishing) the challenges, analyzing the information I was confronted with and making informed decisions that would lead me to my clear objective and eventual landing spot.

What is *your* ultimate destination and how do you begin developing your own flight plan? Napoleon Hill once said, "Whatever your mind can conceive and believe it can achieve". First and foremost, you must identify your **Definite Major Purpose (DMP)** by beginning with a thought, an idea or a goal.

Your DMP might include transitioning to a new job or career, starting a new business, living in a dream home, having financial or time freedom, or reinventing yourself completely. Once you have the idea in mind, you must reduce your DMP to writing. Writing it down will cement the goal for you. Remember, *if it is not written, it is not true!* Your DMP can be very specific and should include a goal completion date. To help envision your ultimate destination and imbed the image in your subconscious mind, you should write your DMP in the present tense as if you have already accomplished your goals. Your DMP may look something like this:

> *By September 1, 2012, I am a successful author and have published a series of fiction books; I earn in excess of $20,000 per month; I own an MD500E turbine helicopter; I live in my dream home in the mountains of Colorado; I have enough money to give to charities of my choosing, and I have all the time freedom that I can imagine to enjoy my life with family and friends.*

Now, that's a destination!

Studies have shown that the best way to ensure that an idea becomes part of your subconscious mind is to read what you have written over and over again until you can actually visualize it in your mind and *feel* the experience when you think of it. (*What does it **feel** like to be living in your dream home? What does being a successful business owner **feel** like?*) This practice sets your intention.

Not many people can formulate a long range plan of action without the support and assistance of others. Now is the time to ally yourself with a group of as many people as necessary to help you *create* and *carry out* your plan. This group will become your **Mastermind Alliance**. Think of this group as your *flight crew* whose combined experience, knowledge, education, creativity, imagination and abilities will help you develop your flight plan and keep you on course throughout your journey. The plan will be your joint creation with every other member of your Mastermind Alliance.

You should schedule time to meet with your Mastermind Alliance at least twice per week until you have perfected a plan of action. Keep in mind that not all plans work successfully the first time. If your plan is not practical and workable, then replace it with a new plan, as many times as necessary, until you find a plan that does work. Each new plan is simply a course correction! *Persistence* becomes a key component in creating new plans when previous ones fail.

Confucius said, "Men's natures are alike; it is their habits that separate them". So, with this thought in mind, the next step is to begin a series of definite, practical actions (navigational tools) that will assist you in forming new habits...habits that Napoleon Hill found to be incorporated in the lives of most of the successful people he studied in the early 1900's. These actions incorporate tools that, consistently put to practical use, will help you reach your destination. These tools consist of **Service Cards**, **Affirmation Shapes** and a weekly action plan guide referred to as **OATS (Objectives, Actions, Time, Schedule)**.

Service Cards are, in essence, promises to yourself to accomplish tasks that you and your Mastermind Alliance feel are necessary in order to attain your goals. They should become part of your daily routine.

You will begin by writing your DMP on one side of an index card. This is done so that you can always keep your destination in mind! On the other side, near the top, write the words, "I promise to". In the center of the card, write down the task or action that you must accomplish. Include a definitive date for completion of the task. Near the bottom of the card you will write "I always keep my promises". Sign and date that statement to affirm your contract with yourself.

One of the most important practices related to your Service Cards is to read both sides to yourself aloud—and with *enthusiasm*—several times during the day, every day. Make it fun and make it a habit!

I would encourage you to start by making Service Cards with simple tasks that you are sure to complete such as "I Promise to: wash, fold and put away laundry by Friday, March 26, 2010". This ensures that the habit of completing your Service Cards is well established.

The next tool that you will design is what I refer to as an **Affirmation Shape**. These are simple, colored shapes such as stars, diamonds, triangles, hearts, etc. to which you affix a personal, positive affirmation which mirrors part of your DMP or is essential to completing your journey. Much like your Service Cards, your affirmations should reflect a specific date in the future by which time you expect your goal to be realized. For example, on a yellow triangle shape you may write: "I own my dream home in the Colorado mountains by September 1, 2012".

Cut out these Affirmation Shapes and place them in highly conspicuous places around your home where you can see and read them multiple times per day, thus reinforcing your destination plans on a regular basis. You'll find that these affirmations will eventually become part of your subconscious mind simply by seeing a colored shape around your home. Change the location of your Affirmation Shapes every so often so as to sustain your intentions!

Most people don't plan to fail, they simply fail to plan! So, we must make and adhere to a weekly, written plan of action (**OATS**) in order to achieve our DMP. **OATS** consist of:

- **O**bjectives (main goals to be accomplished during the week)
- **A**ctions (what actions are required to meet your objectives)
- **T**ime (allotted to accomplish each action)
- **S**chedule (the difference between knowing what to do and doing it; in other words, *schedule it on a specific day with a specific time!*)

You can design a form for your personal weekly use on a home or library computer. You may want to include reading your Service Cards several times per day under the Actions section. Plan to fill out your OATS form every Sunday night for the coming week and then use it!

Once you have developed a flight plan, made your necessary course corrections and established your new habits, you'll find that the journey to your destination is well under way. Just as I did flying police missions, you'll be able to rely on all of your skills and training, accept the challenges you face and you'll be able to make informed decisions that will lead you to *your* eventual landing spot. None of this is possible if you don't *begin with a destination in mind!*

About the Author and Her Sparring Partners

Gina Keeven has worked in the sales and service industry for the last decade. She has a drive rarely found in professionals in her field; and her willingness to take risks has brought her numerous opportunities for both an active career in sales, as well as prestigious memberships in various community groups. She is a hard-working professional, the backbone of any endeavor she takes part in and a strong woman whom many look up to. She prides herself on her tenacity and her ability to build strong sales teams, which provide top quality service for her clients.

Gina continues to oversee the family business, Choices Catering Brokerage (ChoicesCateringBrokerage.com), selling catering and banquet services for many different restaurants throughout the St. Louis area. She has made numerous television appearances and hosted local radio talk shows. Gina is also a frequent guest speaker and event coordinator for community organizations and non-profit groups.

Gina and Mixed Martial Arts World Champion, Jermaine "Bam Bam"/"The Product" Andre, deliver the "GO TEN" message through keynote speeches, corporate sales trainings and weekend workshops. Their high energy, knock-them-into-their-senses presentations have inspired everyone with the courage to "GO TEN Rounds" with them. Together they have the power to "knock your business into action" or help you "knock out bad behaviors" which are adversely impacting your life.

More recently, Gina joined the Gambling Balance Team as its National Sales Director. Gambling Balance (GB) is a world-class platform for shifting the paradigm of how the gaming industry, mental health professionals and gaming enthusiasts approach responsible gaming initiatives. Gina, who is a long-time friend of GB founder, Linda Fitzgerald, has been privy to the formation of the Gambling Balance concept over the past few years.

Gina lives by the words, "Every failure, obstacle or hardship is an opportunity in disguise". (Mary Kay) She has had many obstacles in her career and has met every one with strength, proving to herself and those around her the truth in those words. She has built a successful career providing valuable services to the community and hopes to expand that impact to the world platform of "Going Ten" and Gambling Balance (GamblingBalance.com).

"GOING TEN" with
My Girlfriend, Gina

By Gina Keeven

In a chapter about life mission and goals, you're probably expecting a call to a greater purpose. You may be anticipating an ethereal, delicate, highly-refined plea to embrace philosophical principles. But I'm "kind of a high octane gal"...passionate about life and super fueled for success! So we're "gonna take the gloves off" and go 10 rounds...for the purpose of igniting YOUR passion, YOUR purpose and YOUR success (however YOU define that).

What does it mean to "Go Ten"? Martial arts experts and boxers get into the ring and go ten rounds to demonstrate their expertise and claim their victory. For a business professional, "Going Ten" means going the distance, not stopping short, doing your best and being willing to do it again and again. "Going Ten" means facing the challenge and fighting back. It means reaching your greatest potential and being willing to push past anything holding you back. "Going Ten" is NOT about reaching perfection; it's about doing what is "perfect for you" at this moment in time...with the goal of igniting YOUR passionate purpose.

It's time to "Square Off"
I'm presenting you with ten rounds of questions and directives. They are designed to stimulate thought and help you initiate actions. Make notes and record your responses, then turn your intentions into an action plan!

Round #1 – STOP Thinking Small
It's time to stop thinking small. It's time to be a champion!

Ask Yourself These Questions

- How have I been acting small?
- Where is this manifesting in my life?
- Why act small; how has this benefited me?
- Have I been "blending into the norm" and not living fully?
- Have I defined my dreams and aligned them with my values?
- Am I willing to take well-assessed, managed risks?

Somewhere in this equation you must strive to find the "why" about "what" you are choosing to do.

Round #2 – Have a Business Mentor or Personal Coach

Every person should have a trusted confident, personal mentor or professional coach. Ask yourself these questions:

- Who do I currently look up to in my personal life?
- How frequent are my contacts with that person?
- How would increasing my contacts with that person enrich my life?
- Who has been a role model for me in my professional life?
- What books am I reading that support my purpose?
- What networking groups do I participate in?
- Do these groups strengthen my personal resolve and propel me to positive actions?
- How am I holding myself accountable?

Round #3 – Say "YES" to Your Good

It's time to ignite your passion and welcome the adventure.

- How often do you say "yes" to your good?
- Do you have fun with all you do?

- Are you turning down the "GOOD" that is trying to come your way...by saying "NO" to opportunities?

- Are you trying to "drive the dream" with the brakes on?

- Is it "my way or the highway" with you?

- Does it have to look YOUR way?

- Are you open to having it "look" or "be" another way?

- Are you staying WIDE OPEN to your good?

- What are you willing to do differently?

Round #4 – Fuel Yourself with Confidence

It's time to take a turn towards your good! A mastermind friend of mine often says: "The shortest path towards your objectives is a step in that direction". Keeping your goals in mind and working towards them will bring positive results. Sounds simplistic...but consider:

- Are you walking/working in the direction of your dream?

- Do you give your dream; "lip service" or "sweat equity"?

- How passionate are you about your purpose?

- Is your purpose based on helping others or contributing to the greater good?

- Are you letting the "Power of the Purpose" fuel your dream?

- Are you "Programmed for Success" and taking positive steps in the direction of your objectives?

- Do you take the time to define your goals and establish rewards for achieving specific benchmarks?

- Do you use vision boards and visual stimulation?

- What can you do to build your courage and strengthen your resolve?

- Are you using positive affirmations?

- What are you doing to develop the mindset of a winner?
- How can you emulate others you admire?
- Can you "fake it until you make it"…telling yourself you are everything you need to be?

Round #5 – To Build a Dream It Takes a Team
- Are you struggling by YOURSELF?
- Are you the "Lone Ranger" or "Super-Woman"?
- Why have you not surrounded yourself with supporters?
- You Need A Team to Build the Dream!
- Are you willing to be responsible for the dream and the team?
- Which seven to ten people are excited about your vision?
- What can they do to serve and support you?
- What can you do to serve and support them?
- Set an intention to "invite them to the party".
- Take action on that intention!

Round #6 – Find Greatness in Everyone
- Learn to identify and appreciate other people's strengths.
- Remember that other people's talents can complement yours.
- Fight off the feeling of insecurity or competitiveness.
- Fight off urges of jealousy and envy.
- Switch to an environment of collaboration.
- See beyond the labels and limitations we place on people.
- Find greatness in everyone, and they will rise to your expectations.
- How can you switch your perspectives to expect the best of everyone?

Round #7 – Make Quality Decisions Quickly

- Has indecisiveness ground your business to a halt?
- Do too many options cause you to stall out or tailspin?
- Don't belabor business decisions!
- Let your intuition guide you.
- Gather the facts and make informed decisions quickly
- Weigh your options and then choose the best course of action.
- Make firm decisions, then work to manifest the best possible results from those decisions.
- Be open to adjust your plan when necessary.

Round #8 – Include Fun Events in Your Plan

Do you know why you should include fun events in your plan? Because you want to include FUN in your life! We should all value the moments of fun, joy and laugher that life brings our way. In fact, we should GO OUT OF OUR WAY to create them. Fun and fun-filled events bring great energy to a project. In fact, I am a proponent of "putting the fun in fund raising". There is nothing like fun to energize an idea, motivate a group and deepen the connection you have with clients, customers and business associates.

- Fun, food and good times build better teams.
- Clients, customers and business associates love events.
- Events fuel fun and finances
- Remember to put the FUN in FUND RAISNG

Round #9 – Put Some Snap into It

If you've ever talked to me about a project I'm passionate about, you've seen me snap my fingers. It's sort of a trade mark…(Hey, I'm Italian, I can't help it; I was raised that way). My Dad (Bud Russo) was a wonderful father and a great businessman. Although he has long since passed from this earth, his picture still inspires me everyday to be everything I was meant to be.

- Don't be a "Replica" of someone else's program.
- Be Unique and Daring
- Be Bold, Brave and Bodacious.
- Stand out from the crowd
- Put some SNAP into it!

Round #10 – Be Resolute to be Resilient

- "BAM!"...Did someone or something deliver a knock-down punch to you?
- Have you gone 9 ½ rounds, only to get a knock-out punch delivered?
- What do you do next?
- Have Courage.
- Find Confidence.
- Face the tough times and adjust your plan.
- Be Resolute to be Resilient!
- Start over, if necessary

Things haven't always been easy for me. In fact, my story is full of heart-wrenching disappointments...but that is not where I choose to place my focus. I have learned from the "knock-down punch". I have faced adversity with my health and with my business and battled back from both. As long as I have a breath in my body, I will love and provide for my family, while I strive to make a positive impact in the world. Won't you join me in these intentions for the greater good?

Seven Points of Impact

Point

Personal Empowerment

About the Author

Linda Fitzgerald is an accomplished international author, speaker, personal coach and mentor for those desiring a full, rich, rewarding and balanced life. She has spent more than a decade researching alternate ways to effectively address addictions in the absence of abstinence. Whether you struggle with gambling, alcohol, drugs or donuts, the perspectives in her book can assist you in shifting your paradigm and improving your results.

Linda's comfortable, knowledgeable and no-nonsense style is the benchmark of her training. Although she specializes in addressing problematic gambling tendencies, her work has been expanded to encompass universal applications to avoid addiction through "harm-reduction". She is an advocate of "Self-Help" and "Peer-Coaching" techniques. The broadened version of Linda's work and a "member's only, confidential website" will be available mid-year 2011.

The 4 Aces Linda holds in her signature picture represent the philisophy of: Avoiding Addiction with Abstinence Alternatives.

www.GamblingBalance.com
www.WinYourLifeBackNow.com
www.7PointsOfImpact.com

Addressing Your Addictions

By Linda Fitzgerald

I am not a doctor. I am not a therapist. There is a whole list of things that I "am NOT" or that I have not yet chosen to become. Placing our focus on "everything we are NOT" will never serve us well. So, I invite us to shift our focus to serve ourselves better... remembering that self-serving activities are those which are rooted in survival. Our choices, even those rooted in addictive behaviors, may not always seem beneficial to us; but innately, each choice serves us in someway. Our opportunity is to figure out ways to "do things" which serve our greater good more productively.

Don't think you have any addictions to address? If you've ever "needed" a candy bar, a cup of coffee, a cigarette or "had" to watch your favorite television show or be on social media 100 times a day, this chapter is for you. If you crave the attention of people, if you yearn for a sexual encounter to trigger the endorphins you desire or if you're simply grounded in the "hectivity" of non-stop activity...read on. If you've ever "needed" a drink, a drug, an adrenalin high or fought the urge to gamble, you're going to find this informative and potentially transformative. ***In other words, this information is for everyone!***

We all have addictions (dependence or devotion) to potentially harmful substances or detrimental actions. It is the degree to which we are capable of managing these impulsions or compulsions that will determine their impact in our lives. It is the broad range of these impacts (from mild to devastating) that is the measuring post of our concerns.

First, let us address the issue of whether or not an addiction can be managed. The preponderance of research says "yes"...and sometimes "managing it" means stopping the behavior completely (what is referred to as abstinence). For most of us, one decadent dessert won't kill us; but a lifetime of poor eating habits will take its toll on our bodies. One night of bad behavior at a casino or racetrack is not likely to decimate our finances, but a repeated pattern could erode the stability of our lives. One drink won't adversely affect me, but it could devastate an individual with the genetic propensity for the addiction of alcoholism.

Whose research is accurate? Who should we believe? Can addictions be managed? Are addictions a genetic predisposition, a physiological shift in brain chemistry caused by ingested substances, a cognitive impulse disorder or just a behavioral management problem? All these possible manifestations of addiction are substantiated by documented research. All these aspects exist and manifest differently in the lives of many. More unsettling is the fact that researchers, academics, doctors and mental health experts can't even agree on the complex subjects of addiction, abstinence or harm reduction (also known as moderation or behavioral management). So how do you find your answers?

As I say in my *Gambling Balance* book...***it doesn't matter whose research is right, it only matters how it is manifesting in your life.*** The critical vote is cast by your actions. Which theory do your actions represent? *I encourage you to believe what you do, not what you say. Your hands will always tell you the truth.* Your hands represent your choices. For example: Are you opening a door to a casino? Are you writing a bad check? Are you driving your car to a lover's house to have an affair? Are you lighting up a cigarette? What beverage are your hands delivering to your mouth? What addictive pattern are you repeatedly participating in? Are your hands able to stop? Oversimplified? Maybe...but hopefully useful!

Taking responsibility is the essence of accountability. Personal empowerment is all about taking care of you! Taking responsibility is empowering yourself for the purpose of manifesting "the life you desire and define" by your choices and your actions. Better choices equate to improved results.

I encourage you to know the "what" and the "why" about all your choices. I recommend you move to a neutral playing field where personal actions can be assessed without judgment. Harshness with oneself may be necessary, but judgment does not help

Self-Analysis of Your Behavior:
Self-awareness is the first step towards self-empowerment. Keeping this in mind, we encourage continual self-evaluation of your behaviors and results. There are generally 11 factors to monitor to self-assess and determine if your behaviors have reached problematic proportions. These include, but are not limited to:

Self-Analysis Checklist

1. Preoccupation

2. Developing Increased Tolerance

3. Experiencing Withdrawal

4. Escaping Problems or Moods

5. Needing to "Fix" Problems Created by Habit

6. Lying or Concealing Your Habit

7. Loss of Control

8. Committed or Considered Illegal Acts

9. Financial or Personal Bailouts

10. Jeopardizing Relationships, Job or Education

11. Neglecting Oneself

Ask These Important Questions:

*   What am I doing?

*   How is that serving me?

*   How is that hurting me?

*   What (if anything) do I need to do differently?

These questions will help you get to the root cause of your problem. When addictive patterns exist, there are always "root cause" problems (the real reason we take on addictive behaviors or actions). You don't have to discover the root cause to "fix" the addiction, but you're likely to develop new coping mechanisms until the "root cause" problem is resolved.

You Always Have Three Options:

*   Status Quo—Everything stays the same (I don't need to change or I'm not going to change).

- I'm "IN" and committed to doing it differently (moderation or behavioral management, selective exclusions, balancing techniques, harm-reduction practices, etc).

- I'm "OUT"—I Quit—I'm done with that! I am seeking the path which best supports my decision (going it alone, seeking a coach, getting therapy or participating in group support programs).

We Recommend YOU Take Life-Affirming Actions!

Once you have worked through this process, I encourage you to make life-affirming choices. These can include (but are not limited to):

- Take Better Care of Yourself
- Seek Spiritual Guidance
- Establish a Process for Accountability
- Get Professional Help (Coach, Minister, Therapist)
- Get Group Support for Your Choices
- Stop Chasing Your Tale – Let the Old Story Go
- Let Your Words and Actions Affirm Your Choices
- Address the Root Cause of Your Problems
- Fill the Void – Consciously Replace the Habit
- Be Kind to Yourself through the Process

We could write a chapter on each one of these life-affirming choices...or you could turn to any one of the coaches in this book to help you find answers and strengthen your resolve. In fact, the Seven Points of Impact chapter from my own book was the inspiration for the *Seven Points of Impact* anthology book. It was my desire to give persons struggling with life challenges a place to come for inspiration and support through times of difficulty and change. The important part for all of us is to strive to have a balanced life. When you put your life in order, all things will fall in place. When you put things in place, your life will be in order. It's a life cycle phenomena.

Address Your Addictions:

If you want to "address your addictions", we suggest you turn them over to a "Higher Power". Write them on a piece of paper, specify your intentions for doing things differently, and seal them in an envelope.

Many people have a release ceremony when they "address their addictions" to a Higher Power (God). One type of release ceremony is to burn the envelope in a fire pit. Another is as simple as ripping the envelope up, shredding it or simply throwing it away. You might take this to a minister or mail it to a church...sending it somewhere where confidential prayers would be said over this request. We do suggest, however, that you do NOT keep this envelope. It is the action of intention and release that will begin to form a better pattern for you.

The coaches of Gambling Balance live by the motto: **"When in Doubt—Opt Out!"** We think this is a pretty good guideline for most addictions. Sometimes there is just no good reason to continue a behavior. If drinking, gambling, smoking or other addictive patterns are causing problems in your life, sometimes it's just better to walk away.

Please remember that you don't have to "go it alone". This book was written for YOU. You have been in our hearts and intentions throughout every step in this process. The world is full of people who are willing and wanting to assist you, but you must take that first step...a step in the direction you want to go.

"Reach out in the darkness...and you may find a friend"
Jim Post Lyricist, Performed by Friend & Lover

*****

About the Gambling Balance Book

Ph.D.'s and researchers from across the world have contributed recent studies and authorized works into Linda Fitzgerald's signature book, *Gambling Balance; an Alternative Approach for Every Gaming Enthusiast*. It is Linda's philosophy to strive to "make a difference" in the world and in the lives of others. Her theory is that "everyone knows someone who needs this book".

We encourage you to reach out and make a difference in someone else's life by sharing this information with them.

www.GamblingBalance.com
www.WinYourLifeBackNow.com

Disclaimer – The publisher, LFK Consulting, and the author of this chapter, Linda Fitzgerald are not engaged in rendering mental health therapy or other licensed medical professional services. This chapter is designed to deliver life coaching suggestions and options. The reader is advised to do independent research on addiction and seek professional medical and mental health help as appropriate.

About the Author

Justin Buffer is a Professional Educator and teacher of other classes on educational and personal enhancement. Based in New Jersey, but accustomed to travel, Justin brings his extensive knowledge and his love for learning and personal development to all that he does and to all his classes. His commitment to his and others' individual growth, learning and personal enhancement is the hallmark of his services.

He has a formal education in Political Science, History, Psychology, and Educational Pedagogy and has worked with and taught people of varying ages. You can learn more about Justin and the different classes he teaches at www.justinbuffer.com. He can be reached directly at Justin@justinbuffer.com.

3 Tips Toward Becoming a Maximally-Effective Communicator and Teacher of Anything

By Justin Buffer

There is a good chance that if you are reading this book, you have realized you have gifts, wisdom and knowledge that you would like to pass on and that you want to make a marked difference in this world. Undoubtedly then, you will be taking the role of a teacher more and more. There are three major components that I have come to believe are vital for any teacher, coach or helper to embed into their inner commitment to their own growth, both as an individual and as a teacher. These three components will enable you to grow and flourish as a teacher, coach, healer or helper no matter what content you are teaching and also make continual, maximal impact on your clients and students. Please keep in mind that when I use the word "teacher" in this chapter, I use it very generally. I believe that whether you are a classroom educator, coach, chiropractor, parent, manager or a seminar leader, you are essentially a teacher and must effectively communicate to those whom you help in order to maximize your message. This chapter, then, is really for all of us who are responsible for transmitting information, wisdom and lessons to others.

I have been a teacher and coach for several years. To me there is no greater gift than the opportunity to be a vessel to help someone. Teachers of any kind have the opportunity to inspire, create, transform and help extract what is best in others, shepherding them through doors to greater creativity, insight, and expansion. I have always believed that being a maximally-effective teacher begins with you...who you are...and is usually more important than what you know; because what we know must first come through who we are.

Great Teaching and Communication Tip #1:
Have a Commitment to Truth

A few years ago, a very nice man and I struck up a conversation on the train into New York City. The conversation turned to European history when he mentioned his upcoming vacation tour throughout Western Europe, and I mentioned my own passion for, and study of, European history. The conversation turned to the Protestant Reformation of the 1500's, which is rich with lots of interesting facts and personalities. After he had brought up the name Martin Luther, I commented I had surprisingly learned that the famed Protestant Reformer was an Anti-Semite, authoring a book titled On Jews and their Lies.

The man looked at me, at first with surprise and then with anger and shock. He seemed furious that I had said such a thing and angrily told me that this could not be true. It seemed that I had offended him...perhaps because he was Lutheran or, more likely, because the truth I spoke challenged his core belief system. Although I was not happy that I had unintentionally offended this affable man, *I was reminded again in that moment how protective we all are over our beliefs and perceptions and how we often do not like to hear something that contradicts them.*

Many of us are like the man I encountered on the train that day: We do not like to hear our version of reality and truth questioned, though we often do not see how much our wrong assumptions and close-mindedness to new perceptions impede our growth and enhancement. As teachers and communicators of anything, it is vital that we stay open to truth and new perceptions, new findings, and new research, while not staying stuck in old paradigms or belief systems. Only by doing so can we inspire our students and our clients to do the same...to question their perceptions, to be truth-seekers and to grow as learners.

Great and effective teachers of any kind are great learners and truth-seekers. This principle is the same whether we are teaching American history, personal growth, cosmetology or knitting. *Make truth-seeking and learning a foundation of your teaching, and you and your students will soar into joy and expansion!*

Great Teaching and Communication Tip #2: Committing to Your Own Growth

Only by committing to our own personal growth can we be the most effective teachers we can be. Committing to our own growth means being open to seeing and healing our blind spots, the perceptual emphases and lenses that drive our perceptions and our personal issues that may affect our functioning. As teachers of anything, we have the responsibility of knowing that we are vehicles of wisdom and truth to which others have entrusted themselves. We have a huge responsibility to work on our issues, be constantly bettering ourselves and make sure we are the most optimal, well-running vehicles that we can be. We can only do this if we are regularly willing to look in the mirror and take in feedback for improvement.

Committing to our own growth as teachers and communicators also means using whatever tools are available to help maximize ourselves. We should make every effort possible to walk in to teach and help others with the best that's in us and with as little personal "baggage" as possible. Whether we are teaching teenagers or adults, it will negatively affect learning if we are not dealing with it. *If we dedicate our lives to our own growth, working on our own fears, doubts, and issues that are the core of the personal growth path, we will allow ourselves to be more readied conduits for wisdom, clarity, and truth.* We should strive to walk in to teach and work with others knowing we are a more evolved human being than we were yesterday.

Great Teaching and Communication Tip #3:
Be Mindful of What You Want Taught Through You

Many great transformational, spiritual and seminal texts that I have studied remind us that what is taught through us is usually more important and remembered than what is taught by us verbally. As communicators of anything, we should always ask ourselves what is being taught through us. Are we modeling and teaching positivity or negativity? Are we transmitting hope or fear? Are we reminding others of their goodness or their self-criticism?

"What is the message being taught through me?" is a key question that we should always ask ourselves as teachers or helpers of any kind. When I teach a class on anything, whether it be to adults or teens, I always check in deeply with myself and make sure that I am in a good space, connected to the best and highest in me. In that way, what is transmitted through me will be maximally uplifting and positive. I am always mindful of what I am modeling and demonstrating. *I know that with the gift and opportunity to be a teacher, I have a chance, by bringing forth what is best in me, to remind others of what is best in them.*

www.justinbuffer.com

About the Author

Pat Childers has been helping people her entire life. She truly desires that everyone will know who they are, feel good about themselves, fulfill their life purpose to connect, and know we are "all one". Our life mission is to raise the consciousness for the greater good.

Pat has contributed a chapter in three other anthologies: *Conscious Entrepreneurs: A Radical New Approach to Purpose, Passion, and Profit; The Indigo Children: Ten Years Later; and Stepping Stones to Success: Experts Share Strategies for Mastering Business, Life, and Relationships* with Deepak Chopra, Jack Canfield, and Denis Waitley.

Pat has assisted at many conferences, lectures, and seminars with groups such as Hay House, International Coach Federation, Omega Institute, International Professional Empowerment Coaching, Celebrate Your Life, International New Age Trade Show, New Life Expos, and the META Center in New York. She has assisted many authors as a promoter and a networker and is now ready to become one of the speaker-authors on stage, teaching to the groups herself. She also loves sharing on TV and radio shows, as well as with the written word, and being an intuitive life coach, minister and healer.

Pat Childers, 1022 Roanoke Lane, Marshfield, Missouri 65706
417-859-4963, patchilders1111@yahoo.com
www.patchilders.com

Stepping Into Your Personal Power

By Pat Childers, M.ED, CEC

Everyone has individual gifts that are unique to themselves. It is now time to allow yourself permission to connect with those strengths for good, to enhance betterment and enrichment, and enlighten the world.

It is now time for each individual to look deeply into his or her own heart, mind and soul; and instead of allowing each entity to be in conflict with the other, stop any non-productive diatribes and work together as a team toward achieving goals of happiness and success. The more whole an individual is the better he or she can bring personal empowerment to gift the world, while being open to receive all the love, honor and prosperity that will come back to them.

You are the only one who holds your true "Key to Success". Many people hold the belief, "I'm not good enough". The only way you can let that go is to truly examine your life, and look deeply into what caused you to carry that "mantra" that constantly blocks your success. Did your parents, siblings, organizations, religion or teachers do or say something that BLOCKED you all these years? If you feel that is true, then it is time to examine what you really want, and take the positive steps to move forward NOW. No more excuses, blame or waiting—GO FORWARD NOW!

Sit down in a quiet place, with a notebook or journal in front of you, where you will not be interrupted until you are finished writing down all your hopes, dreams and desires for the rest of your life. You don't need to think about it; just allow a "flowing stream of consciousness".

After completing the list, sit quietly and take some deep breaths. Open your heart, mind and soul to RECEIVE what you wrote. After reading your list, decide on the most important thing you can do NOW for your deepest joy and happiness. Next, make these connections by taking positive steps toward your goals.

As a personal example, I will now share that it is time for me to take a huge step in personal empowerment. I came from a family that was very talented, but held themselves back; because that is what they were taught to do in this world.

An example is my own father, who was in the special services during World War II. He was invited to come to Hollywood by Carl Reiner (Rob's dad) and Alan Ludden (Betty White's husband), but didn't take this opportunity because of what he was taught by the Depression. Instead of allowing his fabulous singing, dancing and acting talents to "shine", he chose to be safe and took a secure job as a purchasing agent at the Terminal Railroad in St. Louis, Missouri.

I feel I followed his example for a long time. I got married on my nineteenth birthday, had two sons, and totally focused on being there for the family. I was active as a room mother, scout leader, sports coach, and then an eighth grade English teacher, who taught her own children, as well as all of their friends.

My objective as a teacher was for each student to feel I truly saw them, heard them, and wanted them to share what they were thinking and feeling, so we could include that into each lesson of the day. I did not send kids to the principal's office for discipline. I took my own breaks to work with them and talk to them, when needed.

Life kept moving on, and I completed my Masters in Education and my certification to teach Gifted and Talented students. All the while I was still being the Mom, who had my sons' entire group of friends feeling they could come to the house for support whenever they needed it.

I enjoyed watching my sons play sports and be in theater productions throughout high school and college. Then they both got married, and I have three grandchildren. I absolutely love and adore them all. They are all individuals with different talents and goals. My objective has always been to assist them in recognizing their strengths and enhance their abilities in all ways. It was a true blessing to me when my grandchildren got to live with me for three years, and I was fully there to assist them with their growth and education. Part of this growth was allowing them to know it is okay, and a good thing, to realize who they are inside and to connect to their highest aspirations, goals and desires.

Now it is time for ME to take another step in MY life. I am NOW "allowing" myself to KNOW that everyone in my family has their own path. If they need me, I will always be there for them; but I do not have to run or direct their lives. They will make the choices for themselves. It is now time to step up toward my own life's goals, desires and ambitions in a way that will be ME honoring ME in my own "Personal Empowerment". This has been a powerful recognition in "acknowledging" that everyone in the family has their own strengths and desires, and everyone has his or her own connective path for living life in joy.

I just returned from a conference where people were crying with emotions and revelations, telling me I was truly "glowing", thanking me for being there for them and for coaching them with my wisdom...wisdom that I've had my entire life. It is now time to OWN these gifts by stepping fully into my TRUE "Personal Empowerment" by turning in my own completed book for publication, which is the dissertation to complete my doctorate, PhD. I am ready to step onto bigger stages, to reach more people, and to assist them in opening up to their own true personal gifts to share in this lifetime. Everyone has a purpose in life...a unique gift or special talent to give to others. When we blend this unique talent with service to others, we experience the wholeness of our own spirit, which is an ultimate goal for life.

True "Personal Empowerment" is showing your love, strength, caring and heart to everyone, so they can learn from you and see it is possible to live a full life every day. It is time for everyone to own their own power to assist the world in healing.

About the Author

Patty Cook, Executive Life Coach, Certified Kolbe™ Consultant and Owner of Life by Design, LLC, has been helping people Transform Stress Into Success™ since 1992, when she successfully recovered from her own "crash and burn".

Sometimes it is beyond our ability to generate the spark we need to get where we want to go, and we need the help of an expert... someone who has risen from the ashes who can help you navigate your way through faster and easier than you can on your own.

A two-time victor over breast cancer, Patty has experienced first-hand how quickly and radically life can change its course and is committed to supporting people in living today like there's no tomorrow.

Patty offers personal coaching, corporate training and keynote presentations, all designed to help people ignite their personal power, so they can achieve their most imaginative goals and withstand life's greatest challenges, creating success from the inside out.

Visit Patty Cook's Life by Design website at www.pattycook.com for resources and programs. You can call 636-861-9100 or send an email to info@pattycook.com to schedule a complimentary consultation.

How to S.P.A.R.K. a Spectacular Life

(From 'Burned Out' to 'Glowing Spark')

By Patty Cook

I now know that we have infinitely more power over our circumstances than we think we do, but that wasn't always the case.

In 1992, after 18 years of working my way up, step by painful step...from a secretary in the estimating department of a major electrical contractor, to an estimator, to assistant project manager and finally earning a coveted project manager position overseeing many successful projects...I just walked away. One crisp fall morning, at the tender age of 37, I walked into my boss's office and retired from the career I had fought so long and hard for and truly loved.

Why? *I walked away because I was constantly overwhelmed, continually overextended, chronically exhausted, and increasingly unhealthy...and absolutely powerless to impact any of it.* I was highly successful by most standards...I had a prestigious job with great pay and benefits, an excellent reputation in my field, a loving marriage, nice car, fun vacations...but my spark was gone. Since I didn't know how to ignite it again, I quit. I was simply burned out.

How could this happen to me? *When* did this happen to me? I didn't have a clue, so I vowed to find out...to discover my own personal power...and then teach others what I learned so they

---

could do what they loved and were good at, without paying such a high price for their success.

My journey from burnout to successful personal coach is a valuable story, but one for another time; because the fruit of that journey is my gift to you today. After years of learning for myself and working with countless others, a pattern began to emerge, forming into five tools guaranteed to generate a spark of creativity.

Laying the Fire

This key concept will help you generate your S.P.A.R.K.: *What you focus on expands.* The more you think about something, the bigger it gets. If you are focused on how overwhelmed you are, for example, you will keep noticing how overwhelmed you are; and the feeling will get bigger and bigger, stronger and stronger, until you feel powerless to change it.

Every situation contains things you can change and things you cannot. Get clear about both so you can stop spending your energy where you have no hope of making an impact, dampening your spirit and eroding confidence. Always identify what you cannot change, so you can keep your focus on what you can.

Igniting the S.P.A.R.K.

S.P.A.R.K. is an acronym for my five tools that have the most impact on helping people shift energy and create positive change. In some situations, focusing on one will be enough. In others, you will need more than one to break free and move forward. Sometimes your issue will be big enough that you will need to use them all. Individually they are powerful; together they are *dynamite!*

Seven Points of Impact

Before you read any further, take a moment to choose one area of your life or work to focus on as you learn. What is dampening your spirit, personally or professionally? What is extinguishing your fire? Where are you feeling stuck? Choose a specific area to map onto this process so the models become integrated, not just "good ideas". There is power in learning the concepts, but infinite possibility comes from anchoring them for use going forward.

Spotlight Success   *"I am the greatest" – Mohammad Ali*
Too often we are off and running to the next thing we need to do; and we forget to celebrate all the wonderful successes, large and small, that we have already achieved. Slow down and appreciate how far you've come; and you will add more satisfaction, fulfillment and inspiration to your life and work.

It is crucial to claim your successes. Celebrate them and even share them with others, because that is your springboard to future successes. When you don't, it's like you don't even realize when you've arrived. You keep striving and striving, relentlessly pursuing the next item on your list, depleting your energy and contributing to feelings of overwhelm. Putting your *Spotlight on Success* generates momentum and gives you more focused energy for taking your life and business to the next level.

Picture Perfection   *"I have a dream." – Martin Luther King, Jr.*
Create a crystal clear vision of perfection for every area of your life: *family & friends; business & career; finances; health; romance; personal growth; physical environment; fun & recreation.* Imagine it all in vivid detail, and express it in language that inspires you. Remember, what you focus on expands, so the more you focus

on what you truly want in life, the more you will find yourself naturally in action to make it happen.

The word "perfection" is used intentionally to encourage you to dream without having to know how you will get there. Have fun with it! Imagine you could wave a magic wand and have it be exactly how you want it to be...for nobody else but you. How will it look? How will it feel? This is where your true power lies. The clearer your vision, the easier it is to find solutions, strategies and opportunities that will fire you up to make it happen!

Achieve Authenticity   *"My definition of success:*
the freedom to be yourself." – Kathy Kolbe
Authenticity is truly your source of personal power. When your life is aligned with your vision, core values, and natural strengths, you are at your peak of productivity; and life and work flow easily. The more you stray from them, the more stressed you become, making you feel tired, irritable, unsatisfied and sometimes even hopeless.

Before you can have that alignment, however, you must know yourself and what truly makes you tick. What values are crucial to your happiness? What vision do you have for your life and work? Why? What natural strengths do you bring to the world? Take the time to discover who you are; then focus on staying true and you will minimize struggle and maximize success.

Remove Roadblocks   *"I think I let go of the need for approval." –*
Ellen DeGeneres
Letting go is a powerful tool for realizing your vision and a

natural by-product of staying focused on what you want. This might include letting go of undesirable people, occupations, obligations, problems, behaviors, attitudes, limiting beliefs, tolerations, attachment to results, perfectionism, and other situations that stand between you and what you truly want in life.

Letting go creates space for new ideas, energy and possibilities to come in, sparking growth and positive change.

Kick-start Knowledge *"An investment in knowledge always pays the best interest." – Benjamin Franklin*
You must invest in yourself if you want to grow, expand and change in a positive way, so always continue to learn and develop. What will it take to bring your vision into reality in the next 12 months? Consider these areas: environments, skill sets, networks, education, body, lifestyle, systems and structures, reserves, communication tools, support structures or even an expert to guide the way. You are worth the investment. After all, this is your life we're talking about!

Sustaining the Fire
Use S.P.A.R.K. over and over again, any time you are struggling, feeling overwhelmed or want to reach a goal but just don't know quite how to get there. Once you regain your spark, your energy and creativity will flow; and you will be well on the way to your spectacular life!

www.pattycook.com

About the Author

 Angela Lieb has been inspiring entrepreneurs to Take Action for over a decade. She successfully launched five executive suite businesses over the span of four years and purchased/sold one of her own. She has been a Business Consultant for a real estate franchise company for the last two years as a corporate employee and has trained thousands of agents on the use of social media in their business. She is the co-founder of several small start-ups and has been the Chairman of the Board for Magnificat Center since 2004. She has been an adjunct instructor at Webster University teaching Entrepreneurship and Small Business and has served on several small business panels and committees. Angela is the mother to four awesome, intelligent children and feels younger today than she did when she was 30. Her passion is speaking and inspiring others to Take Action in their businesses and personal lives. Visit her website at www.angelalieb.com

Taking Faithful Action

By Angela Lieb

I heard a speaker once who said, "Our mess is our message". I thought, "Whoopee, I must have a huge message to share!"

The last three years have been interesting, to say the least. In fact, just about everything I ever made a judgment about or was critical about (either out loud or in my thoughts) I got to experience—and all at once. Isn't that fabulous? I had no idea how many things I judged. For example, if I would visit someone's home or drop a child off at a friend's whose house was really small, I would think, "Gosh, how do they fit in that house? I'm so glad I have a big house. Having your 'dream' house means you've arrived". I now live in a house half the size I did two years ago. How about this one: "How on earth could a parent not know their kids are drinking or smoking pot? They must be totally clueless". Here's one of my favorites: "People who work for a corporation are just scared to go after their dreams". These are just a few of my judgments that God allowed me to experience first-hand.

I have learned over the last several years...through losing my dream business to a large corporation, having my income cut in half, going through a divorce, losing my dream home, moving twice, raising four teenagers, being in debt up to my eyeballs, boyfriend break-ups (rejection), the death of my father, close family members getting DWI's (driving while intoxicated) or MIP's (minor in possession)...that these "messes" build character, test our strength and allow us to learn so we can share.

Through these heartaches and trials, I have learned three very important "ingredients" for staying sane and moving forward. The first ingredient for staying on track, even though your "life train" seems to keep derailing, is to have Faith. Without faith, we do shut down, get depressed and lose hope. Faith—regardless of religion or whether you believe we are guided by God or "the Universe"—MUST be present in order to live the life you were intended. Faith is also knowing that everything that is happening is a lesson and must be experienced for you to learn something, help someone, get stronger or be more creative. I was re-reading one of my favorite books *Happy for No Reason* by Marci Shimoff right after a very devastating break-up; and the book automatically fell open to a page with the heading: "Rejection is God's Protection". I wanted to do the happy dance. I got it! When we are rejected or a window/door is closed in life, it is because He is protecting us from something that would have been disastrous; AND it causes us to redirect our energy to something else. Only if you have faith will you believe that something better is just around the corner—and quite frankly that is one of the only ways to stay sane during times like this.

The second ingredient to getting through difficult times is practicing Gratitude. What this means is every day, multiple times a day, expressing gratitude for the things that are good and right in your life. We cannot expect to get more of the "good stuff" unless we are grateful for the good stuff we already have. If you don't think you have any good stuff or anything going on that is worthy of a "thank you", then start with the basics. Be thankful that you have a bed to sleep in, a roof over your head, your health, your children, your family. Be thankful that you are loved by somebody (surely someone loves you); be thankful for anything you like about your body (i.e., great hair, skin, perfect nose, etc). If you have any income at all, that is something to be thankful for. The next part is to be thankful for even the things that you don't have. *The Secret* book and audio series helped me to learn to be thankful for those things that have not yet happened. For example, "I am so thankful for the endless flow of abundance that blesses and sustains my life. I am grateful that I have $50K in the bank. I am thankful that I have new business opportunities and an expanding base of clients. I am thankful that I have found ways to express my love and our family is living in a house we cherish. I am enjoying life, and I am thankful that I get to go to the beach twice a year and spend lots of time with my kids."

Dreaming or visioning is what some would call "foolish". However, if you do not let your mind conceive of it, then it is not possible. **Don't be afraid to dream!** In order to expand in any area of your life, you have to let yourself dream—that's how it all starts. Practice the exercise of dreaming BIG! Write down your desires. Spend some time thinking and then put them on paper. I believe that we should think of the best possible outcome so we are prepared to receive it. If you are not a natural dreamer, completing this "Take Action Task" from my blog *111 Ways to Take Action in your Life, Business & Relationships* may be a bit difficult for you, but it is important for people who want to grow.

Some of this may sound like "hooey", but it works. We are truly exceptional if we can trust and be thankful for those experiences and opportunities that have not yet happened, but we believe are coming our way. Faith, trust and faithful actions fill the gap between the declaration of our good (our prayers, affirmations, hopes, dreams and desires) and then receiving that good.

That brings us to the final ingredient for getting through difficult times...Take Faithful Action! I remember visiting a friend after her husband had left her. The house was a mess, there was no food in the 'frig, the kids hadn't bathed or changed clothes in days —nor had she—and she sat depressed on the couch. I judged her at that time by thinking, "Just get up off the couch already". Now, having walked through my own personal challenges, I know the pain she must have been feeling. Anyway, I asked her what she was going to do; and she said, "I am waiting for God to tell me what to do". As much as I believe in God and his will for us, unfortunately, he cannot DO the work for us. I have had friends say, "I am waiting for God to send me my perfect mate". My answer to that is, unless he is dressed in brown, carrying a package and knocks on your door, perhaps you might need to get out of the house so you can actually MEET the guy God has ready for you. The same goes for a job. You see people waiting for employers to get back with them after an interview who say, "If it is meant to be, God will make it happen". Well, unless we Take Faithful Action and send the employer a note, follow up with an e-mail or call, then how can we expect that God can help us? He cannot help us if we won't even get up off the couch. There is having faith and believing things will "work out for the best", but along with the faith there needs to be faithful action. You can't control certain situations, but you can control your actions. You can energize the situation with your focus, your talent, your sensitivity, your creativity and your efforts.

Experiencing these trials the last few years gave me insights to where I was judgmental of others, an awareness for which I am now thankful. I believe I needed to learn deeper levels of compassion and empathy, and I will be a better person for having learned these life lessons. However, it is the "ingredients for getting through difficult times" I shared with you that keep me moving forward. There are blind people running organizations, a young man with no limbs who is a motivational speaker, people with cancer getting up every day to get to work—surely we (who have lesser challenges) can Have Faith, Be Thankful and Take Faithful Action during difficult times.

Visit: www.AngelaLieb.com for *111 Ways to Take Action in Your Life, Business and Relationships.*

About the Author

Lynne McDaniel is a Registered Nurse who obtained her Bachelors of Science in Nursing at Southern Illinois University at Edwardsville in 1994. She is a CORO Women in Leadership Graduate. In 2008, she became a Certified Hypnotist. She serves at a local public health agency as a Health Services Administrator and has more than 15 years of experience in public health. She has worked with a multitude of individuals, communities and agencies to address health needs within her local community.

Lynne is passionate about helping people to achieve physical and mental well being. As the mother of three children and seven grandchildren, she brings a well-balanced and loving approach to her inner-child healing work. You are cordially invited to connect with Lynne online at: www.TakeActionTime.com

Healing the Inner Child

By Lynne McDaniel

We are all deserving of a joyous, wonderful, empowered life which is full of healthy, meaningful relationships. Yet many of us had childhoods which weren't ideal, by any stretch of the imagination. Distress occurring during these tender, early days can overshadow all the years to follow. Do you find yourself struggling to form and keep meaningful relationships? Do you see negative habits and patterns in your life and can't figure out why? Is it possible your negative past overshadows the realization of a bright future? If these are your recurring challenges, I invite you to begin a journey of understanding.

Does undertaking a journey of understanding mean unilateral acceptance or complacency? Certainly not! There are many things in the past that often seem unforgivable; but if you don't take action to let go of the negative emotions and habits from the past, they will impact your whole life. Letting go is a process that takes an immense amount of courage and soul searching. It took most of my adult life for me to finally let go of my negative emotions and habits. I think I am finally getting there, but I recognize I will always have room for further growth. A very wise woman told me, "Be the best woman that you can be at this time. Be strong." Over time I became strong...strong enough to continue healing myself and to offer healing options into the world.

Your childhood experiences might simply be marred by parents who didn't love enough or give enough or connect enough. Perhaps you were abandoned by a parent. This type of neglect carries its own stinging memories. Others might have fallen victim to emotional cruelty, strict physical discipline or various forms of abuse. There is as broad a spectrum of childhood experiences as there are children in the world. ***Regardless of your circumstances, you can overcome a less than idyllic childhood.***

Some of my first memories are of a childhood stolen away, through the means of sexual abuse. A trusted member of our extended family was the perpetrator of this atrocity. My parents never knew until I was an adult. Since it started at such a young age, they thought I had a behavior issue. I was an angry, distant child. My mother tells me that I would throw huge tantrums. As an angry older child, I would talk back to my parents and not know when to stop. I didn't realize or care that I was getting myself deeper and deeper into trouble. Since my voice was not speaking the truth, my actions were desperately crying out on my own behalf...yet no one had the ability to solve the mystery and come to my aid.

If you share the painful story of childhood abuse of any kind, then you know that self-esteem suffers. Self-worth and self-esteem erode away and become non-existent. It impacts every aspect of your life. It impacts the people you interact with, the way you talk to yourself, your ability to trust others and your ability to develop healthy relationships.

I especially had issues of trusting men in particular. I remember wondering at a young age why any women would ever want to get married or be in a relationship with a man. When I became a teenager, I thought the opposite. I was looking for love, because I surely did not love myself nor feel loved. I sabotaged relationships, because deep down I didn't think anyone could love me. In fact, most of my adult life, I didn't think anyone loved me other than my children. I didn't feel worthy. If I did something wrong, others didn't need to criticize me, because I was "quicker to the draw" and criticized myself.

I continued to live my life based on the habits and patterns of negative emotions that I developed as a child. This resulted in stress and unhappiness throughout most of my adult life. I also carried guilt despite common sense telling me that I was a small child and didn't do anything wrong. After I divorced my second husband, I knew I had to make some changes, but didn't know where to start. I didn't want to continue to get into unhealthy relationships. Not only had I married abusive men, but I was an active participant in sabotaging relationships. I also avoided forming friendships or relationships of any kind other than with my children and immediate family.

The turning point in MY life was when I discovered hypnosis. The turning point in YOUR life can be when you decide to face the circumstances without shame, without guilt and with a willingness to work through the pain this may cause you. For surely there is a brighter future if you are brave enough to work through this "dark night of the soul." One day I was fortunate enough to stumble upon a "New-Age Store" where Certified Hypnotherapists were holding group sessions. I participated in several hypnosis sessions, on a variety of different topics, and felt wonderful afterwards. I felt a sense of peace that I had never felt before...something we all yearn for and need.

During one hypnosis session, I had a visualization of a sad, lonely and unloved little girl. I spoke with one of the hypnotherapists and was told it was my inner child that needed healing. The minute I heard this, tears sprung to my eyes, because I knew it was true. The little girl in me needed nurturing. Does your inner child seek solace? Does he/she seek the love and nurturing that he/she deserves? My inner child needed to know that I was loved and worthy of love, just as you are. She needed to know it was OK to let go of the guilt. During the course of the next few months, I attended several hypnosis classes and activities. Eventually, I took a self-hypnosis course. Very quickly, I began to feel a change in how I felt about myself. I also made a choice to never use negative self-talk. For the first time in my life, I realized the guilt was gone; and I finally loved myself. I started to really enjoy life and feel happiness. ***I was running my life for the first time, not my life running me.***

I was very passionate about hypnosis, because of the life altering changes I had experienced. Also, as a nurse, I love helping people; I wanted to be able to use hypnosis to help those that had not resolved issues from their past as I had. One of my goals was to become a Certified Hypnotist, which I accomplished in 2008. I am as proud of this as I was to become a nurse many years ago.

I am now in many happy, healthy relationships, including one with a wonderful man. I set boundaries in my life and in relationships. I have several close female friends. I surround myself with strong, positive people, especially successful women who are supportive of me. My biggest lesson has been that you can let the issues from the past run your life forever or you can take action to make changes.

I suggest that if you haven't dealt with the impact of issues from your past, you make a decision to do so and take action now. There are a lot of ways for you to do this. I prefer hypnosis, but guided imagery, meditation, counseling or support groups are good places to start. It may not be the right answer for you at first, but keep seeking until you find what works for you; and set yourself free from the burdens of your past.

About the Author

 Diane Keefe is a Stress Management Coach. Her company, Professor DeStressor, offers stress management training and the Stop Emotional Eating programs. All programs utilize technology which monitors heart rate and teaches the user to get into coherence. As a stress coach, Ms. Keefe will teach techniques that can be utilized to monitor and control stress. She will have you look at what is causing the stress and help you set goals to reduce it. Together, practices will be put in place to retrain your responses for better outcomes. Her goal is to help you take the charge out of stress so you can improve your health.

For more information about stress reduction, contact:
Diane Keefe, Stress Management Coach
"Professor DeStressor"
314-484-8623
www.professordestressor.biz
diane@professordestressor.biz

7 Tips for Taking the Charge Out of Stress

By Diane M. Keefe

We all know that stress is unhealthy for us. Yet, when you feel insecure about your job or someone you love becomes sick, it is natural to react both physically and emotionally. Over half of Americans are concerned about stress in their lives. Too many different tasks many times an hour, such as voicemail, phone call interruptions, emails, instant messages, texting, people requesting your attention and technological challenges cause an individual to stop breathing regularly and feel like their head is spinning.

When stress is not controlled, hormone activity changes by increasing levels of the stress hormone, cortisol, and depressing levels of the vitality hormone, DHEA. You may have noticed that when you are stressed, it is harder to keep weight off your hips and thighs. Your immune system slows down, making you more susceptible to colds and other illnesses.

Stress can impact our health, sleep patterns, communication effectiveness, health care costs, decision making, relationships, etc. How do we cope? The lack of understanding of how to address emotions is the primary cause of today's stress epidemic.

What can you do?

Focus on Self-Awareness

Note when you feel most agitated, angry or frustrated. How do you feel emotionally when you wake up in the morning? How do you react to stresses? As much as 58% of our understanding is due to interpreting the body language of others. Could we misunderstand what the body language is saying? Negative emotions, such as anger, frustration, blame, jealousy, envy (and more) add to your emotional overload. Note how much better you feel when you are thinking pleasant thoughts and projecting love to others. As you give a smile or acknowledge someone else, it becomes mirrored back to you.

Learn How to Stay Neutral and Play the Observer Role

Research reveals that our electromagnetic field can be read in the body of someone ten feet away. This means that our state of mind can affect others around us and theirs can affect us, as well. This could explain why subways, bus stations, airports and other crowded locations can be hard on your nerves. Learn to be neutral. Step back to observe how you are feeling. When you become the observer, it takes the charge out of your emotions. Learn new ways of breathing that help you get your heart and nervous system in coherence to promote better health.

Exercise Your Body and Mind

Twenty to twenty-five percent (20-25%) of the oxygen in your body is used by the brain. It has to pump from the heart. That is the reason physical exercise is so important. Certain times of the day, you may feel less brain clarity. That may have to do with oxygen levels in the brain, sleep deprivation, medications, dehydration and other factors. Take a brisk walk or drink a glass of water to hydrate yourself. Many websites today have brain exercises to help keep your brain working. Play Soduku, do crossword puzzles or read a book. 'Use it or lose it' is still a truism to be noted.

Get an Unbiased Coach

This person can help you look at your life and see where you can focus to reduce negative reactions and improve positive emotions. A trained coach can help you look at your life objectively and will teach you ways to reshape habits for more positive outcomes. You are the only one who can do the work. However, it is very helpful to have someone teaching you new techniques and keeping you on task...someone who has your best interests at heart.

Practice New Ways of Thinking

Negative emotions contain a plethora of impacts for your body, mind and emotions. Learn techniques that help you to neutralize those negative emotions and turn them into positive responses. The mind is far more effective when the emotions are balanced and neutral. Read books by Dr. Wayne Dyer, Dr. Daniel Amen, Cheryl Richardson, Mark Hansen and other psychologists or spiritual leaders who may help you on this path.

Learn Meditation Practices

These practices will direct you to go to your heart for higher intelligence and better breathing practices. Note that when you are stressed, your heart rate becomes irregular; and you may find yourself holding your breath. Practicing coherent breathing techniques (heart and nervous system working in synchronicity) for only three minutes a day can improve overall immune function. Research has determined that the heart's electrical field has 40-60 times more amplitude than that of the brain, and the heart's magnetic field is approximately 5,000 times stronger than the field produced by the brain. More messages are sent from the heart to other brain areas than are going from the brain to the heart. Developing a relationship with your heart will strengthen your relationships, your immune system, creativity and overall health.

Get in Integrity With What You Want in Your Life

Is what you wanted to do in your life in line with what you are actually living? What is important to you? Are you being asked to compromise your values on a frequent basis? If so, it is time to look at what is really important to you; then start taking steps to put yourself into integrity.

You may have to get more training or education; rejuvenate a relationship or let it go. It may involve a move or just looking for more fun and laughter in your life. Remember that as you make these changes, they will impact the others around you, as well. They may have changes of their own. Stay flexible and communicate about what is important to you. Don't make them guess or have to read your mind. The new frontier for this century will involve learning to expand the capabilities of your mind. You may well be on the leading edge for being an example to others. There is no limit to your potential!

About the Author

 Toni McMurphy is a professional speaker, coach and facilitator and has trained more than 56,000 employees in over 220 organizations. She is known as an expert in engaging and inspiring people to bring out the best in themselves and each other in ways that result in meaningful and lasting behavioral change. Toni's book entitled Flowcus will be released in 2011.

Since 1987, Toni has served as President of Infinite Impact, a firm specializing in the design and facilitation of customized, interactive training, workshops and retreats that improve performance and drive results in leadership and team development, employee engagement and enhancing the customer experience. Current projects focus on Sustainability, Teambuilding, Branding and Innovation.

Toni's client list includes Honda, 3M, Godiva Chocolate, Enterprise Rent-A-Car, Air Canada, Wachovia Bank, Eli Lilly, Washington University, and the Missouri Coalition for the Environment.

Toni serves as a personal coach to entrepreneurs and executives and is a Lead Trainer for Phoenix Arises Seminars. She serves on the Board of Directors for Gateway to Dreams and as Advisory Board member for Openly Disruptive. She earned a Master's Degree from Webster University and maintains numerous certifications, including Myers-Briggs and NLP Master Practitioner.

Websites:
Flowcus.com

ToniMcMurphy.com

InfiniteImpact.net

PhoenixArisesSeminars.com

GatewaytoDreams.org

OpenlyDisruptive.org

Breakthroughthemovie.com

Flowcus

By Toni McMurphy

There is a place beyond focus and flow that honors, embraces and maximizes both experiences. It draws upon the very best of what focus and flow each has to offer ... at just the right moment, with the appropriate intensity, in ways that truly serve you, others, the situations you encounter and the outcomes you desire. It is what I call flowcus.

Flowcus actually transcends the integration of focus and flow and serves as a realm where vision and inspiration dance, where possibility and choice intersect, and contribution and results flourish.

Flowcus can be both a noun and a verb. You can have an experience of flowcus or you can flowcus a situation or project. It can also serve as a lens; a vehicle through which you view or examine life's circumstances. Your view or perception can be in or out of flowcus. We live our lives in or out of flowcus.

Life becomes ultimately more effective and fulfilling as you enhance your Flowcus Intelligence (FI) to better navigate, integrate, and transcend the characteristics of both focus and flow with ease and grace. Whether you are seeking to understand your life purpose, managing a project or parenting a troubled adolescent, bringing it into flowcus will result in seeing new possibilities never before imagined and producing breakthrough results you've never before achieved.

Living in flowcus will result in experiencing more peace, joy, acceptance, authenticity and alignment with what matters most to you, including your mission, values and priorities. It won't prevent the bumps in the road that are inevitable along the journey of life, but it will empower you to navigate them with more grace.

Flowcusing means living a life in inquiry that leads to inspired action. It results in exponential, continuous improvement. It requires attention, agility and wisdom. Flowcus invites you to maximize your strengths, navigate your weaknesses and transcend your current limitations.

Flowcus is a journey paved with greater awareness and mindful choices. The first step of the journey is self-awareness. It's helpful to understand your primary approach on the Flowcus Continuum. Looking at the model, identify which side of the continuum you function in most often —the Focus Zone or the Flow Zone. Which list of words best describes you and your approach to most situations in life? Which side of the continuum represents your stronger skill set and your vulnerabilities?

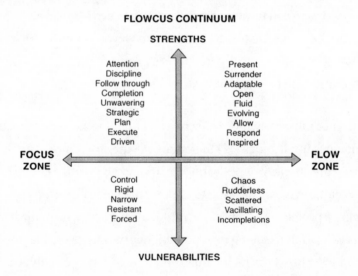

While you will identify with aspects of both the focus and flow zones, it is useful to determine which zone represents your Primary Approach Zone (PAZ). Your PAZ represents what you're best at and what has been positively reinforced by the external world around you, including family, friends, employers and more.

You are certainly much more than your PAZ; and at the same time, your PAZ will indicate predictable patterns in your preferences and behavior, offering valuable information to you and those who interact with you.

People who frequently approach life in the Focus PAZ are known as Focusers. They tend to live their lives with schedules and set plans and thrive on discipline, order, and structure. The core values of a Focuser are completion and efficiency.

People who frequently approach life in the Flow PAZ are known as Flowies. They relish keeping their options open and tend to be spontaneous and highly adaptable. The core values of a Flowy are freedom and possibilities.

It is also important to identify your Opposite Zone (OZ), which is the zone located on the opposite end of the Flowcus Continuum. The OZ for Focusers is Flow. The OZ for Flowies is Focus. Even though you do things in your OZ on occasion (focusers can feel inspired and sometimes flowies are driven), overall, your OZ feels less comfortable and familiar. Developing greater proficiency in your OZ will help you shift there more easily when it would serve you. We are at our best when we learn to move back and forth, across the Flowcus Continuum, based upon the circumstances we find ourselves in.

One way to validate your PAZ is to notice your experience when you encounter people or circumstances that exhibit the vulnerabilities of your OZ, found on the bottom half of the model. People functioning in the Focus PAZ often experience people functioning in the Flow PAZ as chaotic and out of control. People functioning in the Flow PAZ often experience people functioning in the Focus PAZ as controlling and rigid.

Flowcus invites you to reframe people with a different primary approach as potential teachers, instead of a source of irritation. These "teachers" are often modeling attributes you would benefit from expressing more. Michael Beckwith once said, "Some people are nitty-gritty. Some people are airy-fairy. What we need more of is airy-gritty".

Both PAZs embody positive intention and many strengths. Both PAZs also represent a host of potential vulnerabilities and enormous opportunities for development. Flowcus helps you maximize the strengths in your PAZ without over utilizing them to the point of becoming vulnerabilities. A great metaphor for understanding this is to imagine your favorite song playing in the background. Someone turns up the volume and, initially, you have a pleasant experience; because after all, you love this song. But the volume continues to be turned up louder and louder, until it's so loud it hurts your ears.

People do the same thing with their strengths—turning up the volume too loud and over utilizing them to the point where they inadvertently limit themselves and irritate others. Usually they are not aware when they cross the line between strengths and vulnerabilities, because their PAZs are so comfortable.

Focusers can benefit from learning to let go of control on occasion. Continue to plan and make lists—you accomplish a lot by doing so. But, when something unexpected happens, stretching yourself into the flow zone will translate into you having more peace.

Learn to take more deep breaths. Learn to reframe whatever shows up as life happens. Ram Dass used to practice responding to whatever circumstance he met by saying, "Ahhhhh". This is an example of bringing something into flowcus. Simply notice what unfolds rather than resist. Become curious, not resentful.

I once had a Focuser friend who scheduled time for spontaneity. If every minute of every day is planned and scheduled, you can squeeze out space for new possibilities.

Flowies benefit from adding a little more structure. In fact, flowies quickly discover that a little more stucture translates into having more freedom, one of their core values. Flowies tend to keep their options open until the last possible moment, sometimes letting valuable opportunities and experiences pass them by. Getting an accountability partner who will be loving and firm can go a long way in helping flowies in their quest to complete more tasks and projects.

When you learn to say "no" to some possibilities, it means saying "yes" to something else. I have a flowy client who thrives on possibilities to the point where she is spread so thin she isn't able to maximize any of them. When she had her first child, she realized she was going to have to make some tough choices. She learned that saying "no" to some possibilities resulted in saying "yes" to her son.

Greater Flowcus Intelligence creates greater mastery. Your Flowcus Intelligence Quotient (FIQ) is measured by:

- How effectively you maximize your PAZ (Primary Approach Zone)
- Proficiency in your OZ (Opposite Zone)
- Knowing when and how to apply the tools, perspectives and skills associated with each zone when they would be most helpful.
- Your ability to integrate the strengths of each zone in a way that transcends them to live a life in Flowcus.

To take the FIQ assessment and develop a customized roadmap for bringing your life into Flowcus, visit Flowcus.com to order the book.

Seven Points of Impact

Point

4

Relationships

About the Author

"For every person who might reject you if you live your truth, there are ten others who will embrace you and welcome you home."
— Marianne Williamson

Are you ready for your "Sacred Journey" to begin? Are you ready to let go of old hurts and limiting beliefs that no longer serve you and use your pain as a fuel to transform your life? Are you ready now, to surrender, forgive, and finally BE with Joy? Are you ready to dance with wild abandon and let the ecstasy fill you up to your fingertips?

Sandy Moss is a Certified Professional Life Coach and Massage Therapist. She honors everyone's unique and sacred journey. She works with others to uncover and illuminate their own inner wisdom about who they really are and helps them create a life full of passion and purpose!

You can reach Sandy at:
www.beginmysacredjourney.com
Sandy@beginmysacredjourney.com

"Illuminating the Pathways to Your Inner Wisdom"

My Soul Mate — Me

By Sandy Moss

"I want to know if you can be alone with yourself and if you truly like the company you keep in the empty moments."

These words, written by Oriah Mountain Dreamer in her book, "The Invitation", were instrumental in waking me up from my stagnant life and challenging me to begin my "Sacred Healing Journey." I was guided to the book six years ago as a young wife and mother. When I read the quote above, it felt like the hand of God had reached down from the heavens and penetrated directly into my heart. He pulled it out, opened it up, and said to me, "Sandy, are you ready for the next step? Are you ready for the challenge of discovering WHO you really are and why you are here? Are you ready for Your Journey to begin?" My inner voice said, "Yes", as I answered my call to adventure and took another step along my own sacred journey. My life seemed to be a whirlwind of conflicting emotions, the juxtaposition of deeply engrained concepts; and the years that followed were the most profound, most difficult, most enlightening, and most challenging of my entire life.

The youngest of six kids in a small Midwestern town, I remember sitting in front of the twinkling Christmas tree lights at the age of 10 and dreaming about a feeling that I wanted to experience, a feeling of wholeness and completeness that I thought would come when the man of my dreams sat next to me. It was a deep and profound longing, wistfulness over something I couldn't quite understand at my young age. It seemed as if it were a many-lifetimes-deep yearning for a connection to something or someone bigger and greater than me. As I grew older, I categorized this feeling as the search for my soul mate, that Special Someone who knew me so deeply and loved me so unconditionally that finding him would forever fill me up. Like so many young girls, I was looking outside myself for completion instead of inside, where the true answers lie.

The pattern of longing for something outside of me carried forward into the younger years of my womanhood. It was at this critical time in my life that I made the important decision to marry based on fear, rather than courage and unconditional love. My relentless longing for a soul mate, and the fear of not being able to make it on my own, drove me to the altar. It was thus that I began my own Sacred Journey. It would be years before I reached the understanding that every relationship we enter into is another opportunity to know and love ourselves more fully, and in doing so, be able to truly love others.

During the fabled "happily ever after" years of marriage that followed, I learned the lessons of self-awareness, surrender, and truth. My marriage was rocky, to say the least, and denial was my best friend. I was overjoyed to have two wonderful children, and yet their presence did not fill either the void in my marriage or the longing in my soul. Although my husband provided exceptionally for us as a family, our personal connection was lacking on a multitude of levels. I tried for the majority of our 16 years together to blame that lack of connection on him; after all, I had an amazing connection with my kids, my friends, and my community. I spent years unaware of (and not wanting to face) the truth in front of me: that I was, indeed, responsible for the less-than-stellar relationship with my husband—I was responsible for MY PART of the relationship. There were many things missing in our relationship, but there was one very important thing that only I had the power to find. I finally came to realize that one of the major things missing was ME—my true self, my authentic self, my best self.

I am blessed and grateful that in those dark final days of my marriage, during the pain, isolation and final SURRENDER that happens when there is nothing more left in a relationship, there still remained a ray of personal hope. I heard the small, quiet rumblings of my soul. The voice and Spirit of God, which had been whispering to me all along, now started nudging me more insistently. This wasn't the first time I had heard this voice, but this time I listened to it like I never had before. I was lost and felt like everything I tried had failed. I felt that the rules I had used to live life by were no longer working. In that moment of pain and place of surrender, I heard my own inner voice, the guiding council of Spirit, calling. Choosing to listen to that voice, I found the courage to redefine myself and create the life that I wanted to live...the life that I was meant to live...a life of joy, abundance, acceptance and peace!

I'm not going tell you that the next few years of "listening" to that inner voice were easy. As a "peacemaker" personality type, I had spent my entire life pleasing others and keeping my mouth shut in order to keep the peace. Now, in order to follow my inner wisdom, I had to use my newfound voice and run the risk of displeasing some people. I had to open up, stand up for myself, and speak my truth! Fear of breaking out on my own and dismantling the longstanding, traditional family and religious roles around which I had established my life was, at times, overwhelming. However, through the act of utter surrender, of continuing day after day to seemingly jump off a cliff into the unknown, I was led to a place of boundless joy and renewal!

The little girl I had once been, the one who had dreamed of finding her soul mate, returned to me. I did not marry my soul mate; but miraculously, my time with him DID lead to my finding her. She had been there with me all along, buried under the fear, the limiting beliefs, and the constraints I had placed upon myself. My journey had been hard, yet it had allowed me to find my courage, my compassion, and a sense of purpose that I had not known I possessed. The Sacred Journey I had undertaken led me to my true treasure...my self-esteem, my self-worth, and my self-love!

One of the greatest and most sacred journeys in life is discovering ourselves and getting to know that person deeply, accessing our own inner wisdom, defining our values, and then choosing to live our lives from that authentic place of depth, courage, and compassion. This is the Sacred Healing Journey of learning to love ourselves. This sacred journey is about leaning into our pain and darkness and finding the grace that exists in that space. It is about moving past the question of "why is this happening to me?" and instead asking, "what can I learn from this?" It is about asking, "How can I grow and who do I want to be?" Most important of all, it is about discovering how to use your pain to propel yourself into the life YOU were born to live!

Each and every one of us is called not so much to "do" anything in life; rather, we are called to "Be". We are called to BE our true selves, our authentic selves, our unique and most magnificent selves, and to share our selves with the world around us! The Sacred Journey is a journey of discovery; it is a journey that will lead you to discover the greatest thing in life you could ever imagine...yourself!

About the Author

 Dr. Virginia Trevizo Wells is the president of Organizational Behavior Consulting and Training (OBC&T), based out of Dallas, Texas. OBC&T focuses on guiding small- and medium-size businesses to achieve their highest potential through group facilitation, innovative strategic planning, training and executive coaching. She combines her business experience and her academic research of successful business practices to create customized solutions for her clients.

Virginia completed her Ph.D. in Organizational Systems from Saybrook University in January, 2010. Her doctoral dissertation focuses on the success of Hispanic women in corporate America.

Virginia is passionate about helping people discover their inner strengths and capitalize on them to achieve their goals. She brings a unique perspective to her training, due to her 30+ years experience in teaching, training, coaching and in-depth study of human behavior. She captivates an audience and keeps them wanting more with interactive sessions. She has been called "a dynamic trainer" who possesses a wealth of knowledge.

Contact Dr. Virginia Trevizo Wells at:
214-923-9434
vwjunbug@yahoo

Discover Your Secret to Success:

A Treasure that Propels Your Career Upward

By Virginia T. Wells, Ph.D.

Imagine what your life would be like if you discovered the secret to your success regarding your career. What would you do if you found out that the secret was right under your nose and you just did not realize it, because you were not looking for it? Today, I am going to share with you one of the secrets I discovered when I went looking for the secret to success.

I met an amazing young woman who discovered this particular secret and was willing to share it. I found her when I set out on a quest to find the secrets to a successful career. I decided the best way to accomplish this was to interview successful, professional women who made it to the top, despite all odds. The women I met along the way gave me hope for the new millennium…a generation of courageous women who were as determined as I was to find answers to their dreams. The year I spent interviewing these successful women opened my eyes regarding the secrets that contributed to their success and are available to all of us, although few take advantage if them.

The woman this story is based upon is someone who stood out in my mind because of the various obstacles she encountered from the onset; and yet she still made it. She successfully navigated the waters of turmoil and came out the other side victorious and full of life.

The young woman's name is Maribel; a pseudonym has been given here to protect her privacy. Maribel shared her amazing story regarding her trials and tribulations while climbing the career ladder. What caught my attention was her intense desire to succeed, which led her to be "looking for the right people to set in (her) path". She stated that this was one of the ways she had gotten where she was now. I'm sure you are curious to find out how she discovered this secret. This story is her journey to success and the treasure she uncovered along the way.

When we started the interview, Maribel explained her concept of "looking for the right people", something she conceived when she first started working. ***This "looking for the right people" meant creating a support system for herself and paying attention to the advice given by those in that system.*** Unknowingly, her mother was the first person (treasure) she uncovered, which laid the foundation for her initial support system. Although her mother was a single, working mom raising four children, she still found time to emotionally support her eldest daughter. Maribel recalls, "I would work up to 64 hours a week. Although I was 18/19-years-old...I was very young...and had a lot of energy, it still was a lot for a teenager. My mom was always there. She always had breakfast ready and always had good, encouraging words...just to help get through your day."

Life was not always rosy and full of opportunities; and yet Maribel stated, "The whole focus of my career path has just been staying on course, building on what I have learned, and just staying focused. There have been a lot of let downs and a lot of times where my spirit was dampened or hindered, but I've learned to pick myself up and continue the course. When you continue to work hard, there are people that are going to come to your rescue to support you. But it's also about looking for the right people to set in your path."

So as you can see, Maribel realized at a young age the importance of creating a support system.

Maribel continued on her career, and soon she got married. When I asked her who was part of her support system, she replied, "My husband most importantly! My husband of 16 years; we have been through the 'thick and thin' throughout both of our careers." He was the second piece of treasure she uncovered as she traveled up the career ladder; and she was fortunate to have him at her side, because she was soon to face a difficult decision.

The true test of her resolve came when she decided to start a family. Maribel soon realized that the company she was currently working in would not allow her to work and have children. In fact, she stated, "They're still of the mentality that a woman's place really wouldn't be in the workforce if you're going to want to start a family. They are very paternalistic and do believe that you should stay home and take care of your kids. With that mindset, I knew I was not going to be able to continue a career there that contained growth potential. So I decided, once again, to go back out into the workforce, and then that's when I came into the health care industry."

This was a blessing in disguise; because it allowed Maribel the opportunity to, again, strengthen her support system. This opportunity turned out to be fortuitous because of who she met when she changed companies.

Maribel recalls how she felt the day she arrived at her new job. She states, "Almost immediately, I became passionate about the industry and the servicing end. I saw an opportunity for me to become an advocate and educator in that field. Although I was just an assistant, day number two on the job I went and spoke to one of the servicing account managers; and I started picking her brain...you know, 'What do you enjoy so much about your job? How is this done?'

Although she kept telling me, 'This is a very tough job. It takes up a lot of your time', and this and that, I still became infatuated with the position. I told her...I asked her...if she could help mentor me; and I wanted her to teach me the ins and outs of the industry, because that's what I wanted to do. I wanted to have a position like hers someday. She immediately accepted and took me under her wing; and here I am almost 14 years later, still as enthused and as passionate about the industry as I was Day Two on the job."

So you can see that, once Maribel decided to quit her job, she encountered a better opportunity; and she uncovered another part of her treasure, a colleague who was willing to mentor her and provide her support in the new industry. Her decision was confirmed that this was the right job when she met this workplace mentor. She states, "Throughout my career it has always been that challenge of chance. You know, do you take that risk; and how successful are you really going to be at it, what are the downfalls?"

Although Maribel was content in this job, a few years later, another company approached her; and she realized that she was ready for a change. It was at this point that she uncovered another part of her treasure...a supportive boss.

"I think, for me, my current boss is amazing. One thing I have credited to him is he has never seen me for the skill set that I have today. He has always seen me for what I could potentially be, and that gives you an amazing confidence. That gives you a confidence that, trust me, no education in this world could ever provide you. I have always told him 'Some of the best lessons I have learned in life, I've learned them from you.'"

That supportive mentorship is a treasure in itself. Maribel and countless others often pay thousands of dollars for formalized educations; yet it cannot replace the value of a solid support system and professional mentorship.

About Sandra Yancey

 Sandra Yancey is an award winning entrepreneur, international business owner, ABC radio show host, author, movie producer and philanthropist who is dedicated to helping women achieve and succeed. She is the founder and CEO of eWomenNetwork, the #1 resource for connecting and promoting women and their businesses in North America. CNN featured Sandra as an American Hero for her role in mobilizing much-needed resources for the girls' high school basketball team of Pass Christian, Mississippi, in the wake of the Hurricane Katrina devastation.

Sandra is the recipient of numerous business awards, including Excellence in Leadership from the Euro-American Women's Council in Athens, Greece, the Entrepreneur Star Award from Microsoft, the Woman Advocate of the Year Award from the Women's Regional Publishing Association, Women Advocate of the Year from *Enterprising Women Magazine* and, most recently, the Distinguished Women's Award from Northwood University.

Sandra is the author of *Relationship Networking: The Art of Turning Contacts Into Connections* and is featured in *Chicken Soup for the Entrepreneur's Soul,* which showcases some of the top entrepreneurs in North America.

The inspiring and motivational movie she produced, The GLOW Project, features prominent corporate achievers and successful entrepreneurs who share how they manifest, unleash and expand GLOW to achieve incredible successes (www.glowproject.org).

Central to Sandra's commitment to serving others is the eWomenNetwork Foundation, a registered 501 (c) (3) non-profit that supports the financial and emotional health of women and children in need. Since its inception in 2000, the Foundation has awarded hundreds of thousands of dollars in cash grants, in-kind donations and support to women's nonprofit organizations and emerging female leaders of tomorrow.

Sandra holds a Masters of Science degree in Organization Development from The American University, Washington D.C. and a two-year, post-graduate certification in "Organization and Systems Development" from the prestigious Gestalt Institute. Sandra is married and has two children.

www.eWomenNetwork.net
www.eWomenNetworkFoundation.org

About the Author

 Linda F. Kluge is the President and Founder of LFK Consulting, a company that specializes in authoring, publishing and promoting personal empowerment materials. If you are an aspiring writer, published author, personal coach, business mentor, spiritual guru or everyday philosopher who has something inspiring to say, we encourage you to write in our anthology book projects! We believe in giving value to the reader, while opening an avenue for services and revenues for the participating authors. Our live events and members' website serve as a benefit to all who come seeking. Contact us for more details at: www.7PointsOfImpact.com

A Tribute to Sandra Yancey

Founder & CEO e-WomenNetwork

By Linda F. Kluge

I met her on what was suppose to be an uneventful
Thursday evening...Sandra Yancey, the founder and CEO of
e-WomenNetwork. I was at the local event with the purpose
of business networking and moving my company's projects
forward. She had flown in from the Dallas, Texas, corporate
headquarters of e-WomenNetwork, to speak that evening. That
was all that I expected; a lovely dinner, a keynote speech and
maybe a great dessert! Little did I know that Sandra had other
plans for the evening. She had come to town with the goal to
inspire, motivate and empower the women in that room to affect
changes in the world, by altering their approach to "business
as usual". How was I to know she would change my world that
evening?

While I patiently waited for the salad to be served, an air of
excitement was permeating the room. Who was this woman
whom everyone was clamoring about with such great
enthusiasm? My interest was piqued, and I began to read
her profile in the evening's program. Being fairly new to the
e-WomenNetwork, I was unaware that Sandra had grown
the organization to 90 chapters throughout the United States
and Canada, hosting a database of more than 500,000 female
professionals. Impressive, I thought, and then I read on. The
e-WomenNetwork website was ranked #1 by the Business
Women's Network organization, making it the best online
community for female business owners and professionals in

North America. As such, it is the most visited women's business website on the World Wide Web, receiving more than 200,000 hits daily. The notable facts and figures of her accomplishments raised her to new stature in my own mind, and I began to understand why others waited impatiently for her keynote address. Yet, it wasn't until she spoke that my true admiration was solidified; and I got a glimmer of her greatness.

As she spoke to the gathering of women that evening, I saw the synergy in our life's purpose. My heart warmed as if engulfed in a blanket of hope. Could it be that, instead of competition, collaboration would be a better stance to take? Didn't it resonate with my own values to "give freely" to others, without concern in how it would return back to me? I had always proclaimed to live by the slogan, "You can't out-give God"...but was I really implementing that philosophy within my business? Were my professional actions truly in alignment with these values?

I listened intently as Sandra ran a 20 minute "boot-camp" for aspiring and established entrepreneurs. She spoke not only of ways to support and uplift other business women, but also on the basics of networking protocol. Inspired by her words to the gathering that evening and greatly enamored with her success, my inner being yearned to know her better. Then it came to me like a lightning bolt; invite her to participate in the anthology book I was compiling! If she participated, others would be attracted and the project would have success.

My old patterns crept in. I was focusing on how her affiliation could benefit me. At that juncture in my life, I was struggling to overcome a year riddled with hardships cumulating from my husband's debilitating illness, the loss of both our jobs and the subsequent ensuing economic hardships so many Americans have faced during this decade of challenge. When traditional employment seemed ever illusive, I formed a business to author, publish and promote personal empowerment books. I was compiling our first anthology book with the intentions of inspiring, motivating, and guiding the world towards positive change. My goals were lofty, while my financial situation remained distracting. We were burning through our savings at an alarming rate. The book was just a dream taking shape; a concept burning deep within my desires and an avenue for revenues, which my small business so desperately needed. My focus shifted to my own financial survival and to moving this project forward. It was Maslow's hierarchy in full force. If I could interest Sandra in the project, others would be attracted and we would have success.

I waited in line while others talked with Sandra and I geared up for "the pitch." It was a long shot, but one I needed to make for the sake of my business. Sandra had made herself so approachable that I was not afraid to introduce myself to the woman so many put on a pedestal (a place she tells you she does not want to be). She stood patient and attentive to each person speaking with her. When it was my turn, she gave me that same full measure of her attention. Considering her stature in the community, I was a little surprised, but overwhelmingly pleased at this. I introduced myself, quickly explained the anthology book concept and invited her to write a chapter. She applauded our intentions and suggested I interview her for the project. Before I knew it, I was holding her personal business card with the handwritten name of her administrative support person inscribed on the back. She had given me a private email for my personal use and access to her. She had said "YES"...and I wondered how it happened! I dared not question it. I dared not even breathe or the magical spell might be broken. She had said, "YES"; and I walked away in shock!

Little did I know that my life lessons from this simple meeting would be so enormous. I had heard her speak of uplifting other women, of giving first, without monitoring to see what was in it for you; but I had never experienced anything like this. It was synergy and networking in action. Up until that very moment, it had all been lofty words and high ideals, which I wanted to fully embrace; but I was tainted from years of struggling in a harsh and demanding business world. Most of my professional career had been spent in commission-based sales work. It was truly a man's world, with few women allowed to participate. My exposure had changed me from the soft and gentle person I was raised to be into a highly aggressive competitor, all justified for the sake of providing for my family.

In the ensuing weeks, I prepared for my interview with Sandra by familiarizing myself with her book: *Relationship Networking: Turning Contacts into Connections*. I was nervous, not of the task of interviewing her, but concerned, rather, that the "magic bubble" would burst; and she would withdraw her willingness to participate. The enormous ripple effect her affiliation with our book had created was just as I had anticipated. Her celebrity status as a "public figure" in the women's networking community carried weight far beyond my own influence on the project. What would happen if she withdrew? What would happen if she didn't follow through? As I worried and fretted for my small business, I continued to read her materials, gaining a better understanding of the "bigger picture" that motivated this great woman.

The tide really turned for me when I listened to the audio CD of Sandra's *Relationship Networking* message. Her gentile mannerisms and savvy business acumen clearly came across. There was shrewdness in her message, tendered with hospitality and grace. Her words on collaboration resonated with my own life's philosophy. My awareness of her life purpose expanded, and I began to relax into the knowledge that she really did want to help me. In the macrocosm, she wanted to positively impact all female business owners and entrepreneurs; and in the microcosm, that is accomplished one woman, one family, one person at a time.

We spoke on the telephone and, later, in person when I flew down to the corporate headquarters. I pressed for information that would help me understand how she had evolved into such a strong businesswoman with an impassioned fervor for the cause of "fempreneurs". Sandra talked of values imparted by her mother. We discussed the "wisdom of the ages" that had been passed from one generation to the next. Slogans, such as, "Give without remembering, take without forgetting", were discussed. I soaked it all up like a sponge...for my desire was to make the shift into a higher consciousness demonstrated through greater deeds and an elevated life purpose.

She had built the vessel of e-WomenNetwork like a magnificent sailing ship, with mast and sail strong. She stands at the helm, gently steering the rudder, to stay, guide or correct the course. We women at e-WomenNetwork are the gusts of wind she captures in the sail. We are the gentle breezes that blow the winds of change. Together, we move the rights of women forward...holding steady and true to our intentions of positive personal change...while also helping men who affiliate with the organization. We lovingly call them "e-males".

I've come through this process a changed woman, better prepared to run my independent small business. I have released the tendency to be cautious, tainted or suspicious. I understand that I can have strength without aggression or competition. I now think the best of people, understanding that they might just be who they represent themselves to be. I've matured enough to know that, even if they disappoint me, I am better served to just love them in return. I know that to possess wisdom is a far greater value than just having knowledge. I expect greatness to come from simple acts of kindness and generosity...and I am motivated to do more and be more in this world.

Sandra's personal philosophy to "lift as we climb by helping others along the way", and the influence of e-WomenNetwork are destined to resonate throughout the remainder of my professional career (and beyond). Our small publishing business has now sponsored a dozen women, helping them to fulfill their dreams of becoming published writers. We barter for services, whenever possible, for the sake of establishing "win-win" situations for everyone. We give more than we look to receive, and we're networking our contacts into connections. Business is booming and life is good. How can the words, "thank you", be sufficient? I'll just have to trust God to love and bless this woman throughout all the days of her life. Think I'll network to a "Higher Power" and a few angels to make sure that is accomplished!

About the Author

Donna Gamache is an accomplished speaker, mentor and Personal Business Strategist. For the past two decades, many business organizations and savvy business leaders have turned to Donna and Donna Gamache Global for guidance. Through her leadership as the Executive Managing Director of the Greater St. Louis Metropolitan chapter of eWomenNetwork, the fastest growing female membership networking group in the nation, resources are offered that engender women with the skills needed to be successful business leaders in today's changing economic climate.

As they say on the "Gamache Panache" radio show, Donna brings passion to everything she does. Her *mission is to help you define who* **YOU** *are on the inside so you can reflect that on the outside.* **Knowing** *your personal style and integrating it into the way you dress, communicate with others and do business will give you the confidence to ultimately attract more clients and produce greater revenues.* A wealth of additional information and video examples are available on www.DonnaGamache.com.

Donna is a dedicated wife to Stephen Gamache, owner of Stephen Gamache Photography of Webster Groves, Missouri (www.SGPhotography.com). Together they help perfect the brand image you desire for your company, while gaining the competitive edge you seek.

For additional information and useful tips, please refer to: www.DonnaGamache.com

Reflecting Your Authenticity From the Inside Out

By Donna Gamache

"To thine own self be true..." William Shakespeare

The ultimate relationship we have is our connection with God. When we ground ourselves in His grace, living by faith, we prepare ourselves for the great adventure of life in which we are participating. This is by far the most important aspect of a well-lived, successful and harmonious life. From that starting point, blessed with free will to exercise our own choices, our next most important relationship is that with our authentic self. By knowing our unique gifts and talents, we can help others be more successful in life and business.

A woman's relationships are woven as intricately as the garments with which she adorns her body. In this complex day and age, there are multiple layers of relationships we cultivate as modern women. No longer are our relationships bound exclusively to home and family. They stretch ever outward to the local, global and virtual communities. We are daughters, sisters, wives, mothers, grandmothers, teachers, mentors, friends, business owners, executives, and entrepreneurs; and those who "want to have it all" are called to adapt.

Business management is growing in its complexity, particularly in today's environment where mergers, acquisitions, downsizings, world events, a volatile economy and ever-shifting market trends demand focused, informed and proactive approaches. Never before has the competitive struggle to succeed in business been so great. Never before have the opportunities to achieve phenomenal success been so vast. The economic landscape today is fertile and awaits entrepreneurial women who, when tooled for the "right results", can be as competitive as any male counterpart. The secret is to know yourself and define what you want, while looking and acting in congruence with your personality and values as you travel the journey of accomplishment.

As a Powerful Business Presence strategist, I predominately work with women to help implement a host of tools for success. In collaborative boards, networking events and private meetings, we help women mature their business concepts and personal branding towards optimal success. You must know yourself and your heart's desires, so that we can help you define the right steps for implementation.

Business Networking and Leveraging Relationships

Entrepreneurs and savvy business women (and men) have learned the value of professional relationship networking. Organizations, such as eWomenNetwork, serve as a valuable community resource, helping women in business connect on meaningful levels, demonstrate their talents, share their expertise, and showcase goods and services. In addition, they learn to handle a wide variety of everyday issues often facing small businesses. The paradox is it's not what you RECEIVE that makes the networking valuable; it is what you GIVE that enriches your professional relationships... as you become the blessing for others. This "lift-as-you-climb" mentality for leveraging relationships and assisting others seems a natural fit for today's business woman and community leader.

Networking organizations serve as a natural incubator for the aspiring entrepreneur. Many women find themselves thrust into independent businesses due to economic necessity. Others bravely run the gauntlet of business after making the choice to follow their dreams and passions. Often times, the inexperienced entrepreneur is unprepared to immediately excel within the process. This is where speakers, personal coaches, mentors and friends help polish the stone into its shining presence.

Build Your Powerful Business Presence!

Having a Powerful Business Presence tells the world you mean business! **Every interaction you have with a client, prospect or colleague either works in your favor or against you when it comes to creating a Powerful Business Presence.** Do you have it? Do you want it? How would it impact your bottom line? Being deliberate about your business presence helps you soar above your competition! You have only three seconds to make a positive impression... in person or online! You will want to maximize your initial impact through the development of your personal brand and style.

Your branding relates to how your business shows up for others. It is the consistent message, color, style and genre of your presentation. It is business cards that stand out, web sites that impress, and one powerful, reliable public appearance for your emerging company.

Discover Your Personal Style!
To maximize your initial impact, we encourage you to align your personal style with your professional vision. Moreover, this style... your style... deserves to be an authentic expression

of your personality. A Powerful Business Presence exudes confidence in personal style, posture, etiquette, leadership and verbal and non-verbal communication skills. You will leave a powerful business impression by finding out your true personal style. It will make you feel comfortable and confident in any situation. You will learn to accentuate your best features and camouflage your problem areas.

At Donna Gamache Global, we work with women to analyze their primary and secondary style of clothing. We have defined five major categories and work with women to bring out their best within those style groupings. The important factor is to find the congruency between inner personality and outward reflection, as modeled by the clothing and accessories you select. Although the examples are simplistic, they give you some general insights as to your own tendency towards personality, fashion and style.

Trendy Alluring –
Personality: Vivacious, charming, charismatic, full of life
Clothing Style: Latest trends, accessories with jazz and "bling", open or low necklines

Timeless Classic –
Personality: Grace, warmth, sophisticated, trustworthy, reliable
Clothing Style: Tailored, traditional, simple, understated, conservative

Dynamic Driver –
Personality: Gutsy, confident, in control, intense, savvy leader
Clothing Style: Unusual details, one-of-a-kind boutique dresses, chunky jewelry

Spirited Sport –

Personality: Active, always on the move, enjoys competition, also has an easy-going side

Clothing Style: Athletic wear, low-key jewelry, comfortable shoes

Endless Romantic –

Personality: Caring, supportive, kind, comfort giver, gentle, often soft spoken

Clothing Style: Feminine details, lace ruffles, floral prints, antique jewelry, clutch handbags

Sometimes things can seem to be in a bit of a hodgepodge when it comes to your wardrobe. Your closet may contain a host of outdated or mismatched pieces. Your outward appearance can begin to appear incongruent with the professional image and message you wish to portray. However, after some in-depth work, we find most women will have a predominant style and a secondary, yet complimenting, tendency. When we discover the thread that ties together your individual style, it often cultivates bold confidence within you! As you embrace your unique gifts as a person, you move into greater acceptance and increased confidence. When you dress in alignment with your personality, there is a congruency that validates you as an individual in your outward expression to the world. People begin to feel comfortable in your presence, as your own confidence blossoms; and you start to attract prospects and clients because of your authentic self shining through from the inside out.

For additional information and useful tips, please refer to: www.DonnaGamache.com

About The Author

Danelle Brown is the founder and president of Queen Bee Consulting and a Certified *Book Yourself Solid* Business Coach.

She is also the Marketing Director for MB Tech, Inc., the technology consulting company she and her husband run together. Thirteen years ago, she and her husband started a home-based business, Marcel Brown Technology Services. In part because of her extensive marketing/promotional efforts and the time she spent "learning how the world works", Brown and her husband have grown their company each year through its smart marketing efforts, as well as through client retention and word of mouth.

Using resources from both organizations, she specializes in showing family- and couple-owned businesses how to get more clients than they can handle! Brown is known for turning an ordinary business into an extraordinary one. Danelle has also earned the nicknames "master networker" and "Queen Bee of Connections" in her local geographic and online communities. Brown specializes in coaching, marketing consulting, social media instruction and implementation, as well as hosting business mastermind groups.

Her book, *Soulmate Proprietors—How To Run A Business With Your Spouse And STAY Married!*, will be debuting in February 2011. Visit www.queenbeeconsulting.com to find out how Danelle can help your business become stronger.

Happily Ever After

(How I Manage To Run A Business
With My Spouse And Stay Married)

By Danelle Brown

They say to write well, you should write what you know. This is what I know: I have been married to my husband, Marcel, just shy of 15 years at the time of this writing. I've been running a business with him almost the entire marriage—and we haven't killed each other yet. Many people we meet seem amazed at this fact. So I decided to share my story in hopes that it helps other couples in business.

When we first got married in the early nineties, we both had corporate jobs. But my husband, born with a proficiency in computers and a secret desire for entrepreneurship, started helping people on the side. This soon flourished into quite the little business. But it started taking up a lot of time and left us wondering how long we could keep it up.

Then we had our first child, and Marcel hit me with the fact he wanted to do his business full time. Any sane person would freak out at the notion of quitting a full time job with benefits right when you bring your first child into the world—which I did. But I supported him. So we did what any other naïve and unknowing young entrepreneurs do—started out on a wing and a prayer. We saved three months of his salary and figured if we couldn't pay our bills in three months, he could always just get his job back. (That was possible back then!) Some business plan, don't you think? Our friends and family freaked! We must be crazy! Entrepreneurship is sometimes hard to explain to people who have never owned their own businesses.

I was still working a full time job at the time, so my role in the business was limited to very simple marketing and promotions. I would go to Chamber of Commerce events and tried to figure out the ever-changing rules of newspaper ads, postcards, and direct mail campaigns. It wasn't long before I realized I wanted to have a bigger role in the family business. I was feeling left out, missing out on all the fun things about owning your own business, because I was still working a full time gig. A steady paycheck was hard to give up, especially with a new baby in the house. However, I could not escape the longing to be involved in this wonderful thing we were creating. Just like our new baby, our business was also our baby; and I felt like I was neglecting it.

"Lucky" for me the economy took care of this when they downsized my company. At first I felt sad, but then liberated. Now I could move on to help make our mark in the world with nothing holding us back!

I began to dive face first into marketing, making sales calls and handling all the back office duties to give Marcel more opportunity to be out providing the service. It is amazing the clarity that comes with the desire to eat and pay your mortgage. But at the same time, I was trying to find my place in a computer service company when I had no idea how to service computers. It was like I was constantly trying to prove my worth.

Along the road of discovery come bumps and bruises. Who is in charge of what exactly? We found ourselves stepping on each other's toes, which always led to some sort of mess to clean up. Marcel had a hard time letting go of many tasks that he had always taken care of and letting me take it to the next level. Sometimes they were very costly mistakes, but that didn't stop our ambition. We grew bigger and then opened a storefront. As our business and visibility grew, I soon found myself giving advice to other business owners. I discovered that couples ran many of these businesses! A desire grew in me to help people like us—people who know both the struggles and joys couples who run a business go through. So almost by accident, I became a business coach, started my own company, and now get to help other business owners every day!

I am not going to lie to you. Some of the biggest hurdles in our marriage have been because of the business. We have run into just about every obstacle you can imagine. We have been told our business is high risk, have been turned downed for loans, had to reorganize—you name it. Pick a financial hardship, and I think we have been there. This can lead to many sleepless nights. I've possibly had about three nervous breakdowns; and believe me, sometimes a good nervous breakdown is just what you need!

At first I used to hide my feelings from my husband, but now I know not communicating with him just made things worse. I thought I was hiding my pain, but he was very aware. Once I started sharing my worries with him, he helped me put them to rest; and we became a stronger team—taking on every obstacle no matter what.

But what do you do when you don't know how to become husband and wife again instead of co-workers? This has been, and continues to be, a struggle for me, as well as for many other couples I have spoken with. How do you instantly become a loving spouse to someone who seemingly did nothing but piss you off the entire day?

"So help me, if you even think of touching me after what you did today...!"

At what point do you turn off the day's business activities and turn on the family activities? Many times I have had to remind myself over and over that I love this man, I love this man, I love this man. I have found that you never really do turn it off; you just learn the right time to silence certain voices for the greater good!

Somewhere along the way of this great adventure, I found out not only how much I love working for myself, but also how much it strengthened my marriage. We were so young when we got married that we were already growing up together to begin with. Now we've grown a business together! I can't think of a single monumental task I have taken on without my spouse being involved. This is also what I am finding to be true with the couples that I have interviewed. Across the board they all say, "How could you not run a business with your spouse? I can't imagine it any other way."

I explain all of this so you understand that running a business with your spouse isn't always easy; but in my opinion, it can be a blessing. It is my mission to teach couples how to make the stressful times playful, include their kids in the business, use their particular strengths to divide and conquer, avoid the snowball of crabbiness, and manage the transition from the boardroom to the bedroom.

But above all, I want to teach couples that no matter what happens, keeping the marriage a priority is essential. These small efforts are what lead to the big successes that you reach together.

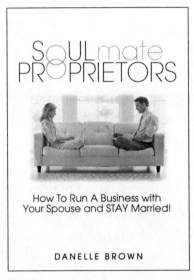

www.SoulmateProprietors.com

About the Author

Becky Schoenig works on an intuitive level with her coaching clients. Whether you are coming to her about your business, your relationships or questioning what it is you were brought to this world to do, Becky can teach you how to open up to your own intuition, allowing your feelings to guide you in your choices. We are all intuitive, but many of us lack the confidence to trust in these feelings. By becoming more confident in other parts of your life, you learn to trust your own intuition guidance even more.

Why work with Becky?

If you are thinking about starting a new business or taking your business to the next level, her creativity, connections, and ideas can take you outside the box.

If you are in a relationship and want to take that relationship to the next level, allow Becky to assist you in having more open and honest conversations with the one you love.

If you are feeling stuck, knowing that there is something more for you but just not sure what it is, let Becky help you to discover it.

We all have the power within us to do, be, and have anything we want. Sometimes you just need an extra nudge or a big old kick in the butt.

Connect with Becky at: www.BeckySchoenig.com

Commit to Your Relationships

By Becky Schoenig

I remember my Mom coming into the kitchen when I was about six years old and telling me she was leaving my Dad and would not be coming back, but that she would be coming back to get my sister and I soon. The pain that I felt seeing my Mom and Dad separate was more than I felt I could ever bare at the time. Their arguing, the bickering, and the dysfunction went on for years. I only remember growing up and thinking there had to be a better way of going about "something like this"...the ending of a relationship, the separation of a family. It was not healthy for my sister or me; and I know, for sure, it wasn't healthy for my parents, either.

I continued to grow up questioning: Is this the way relationships work when you fall out of love with someone? Does it have to turn into anger and resentment? Are families always torn apart? I was painstakingly aware of how relationships could end and people move on. Whether it was marriage, friendship, school relations or business, relationships were something in which I had little faith.

Over time, I've learned love isn't always obvious; it takes various forms at different times in your life. I know for my husband, Jason, when he met me for the very first time in the break room at Gem City College, it was love at first sight. I, on the other hand, was already "in love" with someone else, a man to whom I would soon be engaged. This didn't discourage Jason or stop him from building a deep friendship with me, one that would eventually develop into something more.

I remember the very moment that I knew I had fallen in love with Jason. A very close friend of mine passed away in a car accident. I decided to spend some time at home, and Jason was kind enough to give me a ride to the train station. We talked, and we shared comfortable silence. When my fiancé picked me up to take me home, I put my arms around him and realized that I was wishing it was Jason. The shift was as simple and as complex as that. Now, 14 years later, we're happily married with two wonderful children, our own business, and an incredible life. I know every day how blessed I am to have created this wonderful family with such a loving and caring man. Just like any relationship, there are ups and downs, ecstatic highs and depressing lows; but I still love my husband tremendously and have never doubted the path that I've chosen.

One reason our relationship is so strong is because we have always been very upfront and honest with each other, no matter the consequences. I think our commitment to open communication and honesty occurred because we had built a deep friendship before we had a loving, intimate relationship. So when, over time, just like many other relationships, the spark of him touching my hand or the butterflies that flutter in my stomach went away, we talked about how we felt about that. We talked about the questions that were going through my mind: Is that feeling gone forever? How did we lose that? Can we ever get that back? I missed that; and when I expressed these feelings to him, it turns out we both missed that. This didn't mean that we had fallen out of love with each other, and we knew we loved raising our family together. We both even knew we were still with the one we wanted to spend the rest of our lives with...but what if there was more? What brings that spark back?

I wondered if we could have both: the kind of love that makes your heart pitter-patter and your stomach turn upside down and the kind of love that makes you want to tough it out in the rough times, through the bills, the kids, and the curves in the road. Do they have to be one in the same or can they be from different sources? Now, for many couples, this is when the trouble starts. People seek outside of their relationship; the honesty and trust takes a backseat to affairs and sneaking around. Fortunately, we had always been honest about our feelings. So, after much discussion and heart-to-heart talks, we came up with what works for us and found our "pitter-patter". Through this, we came to the realization that there is no one answer to what love looks like and how we receive love. More importantly, we learned that there need be no limits to love.

I've since found that love can come when you least expect it, from places you didn't know to look. It can come through heartfelt discussions with the one who's been there all along, from a thoughtful gesture from someone you didn't expect, and from a friend who will listen when you need to talk. Accepting the love you have, recognizing the love you need, and creating the love you want is easy. When you express a need, it is answered each and every time. It may not look like everyone else's answer, but it's yours.

I have witnessed the struggle of gay couples, bi-racial couples, and families being judged for how they chose to believe and live. In the past, our society has determined what these relationships are "supposed" to look like; and I believe today we are witnessing people showing that it no longer has to look the way it once did. So, how do you determine how your relationships should look? How much time, effort, and honesty are you willing to invest in your relationships?

Keep in mind, our relationships go far beyond the bounds of our own families. How easy it is to say we have 1,000 or so friends on Facebook or we have sent out 20 tweets today. But the real questions are: Would you take a day off work to spend time with them just because they needed your help? Could they rely on you?

Many of us are small business owners working for ourselves and, seemingly, "doing everything". We hear the same thing over and over; there is never enough time or money to do all of the things that we want to do. Social media and technology has created a great way for us to connect and leverage ourselves on a bigger level, but it has also made it easy to send a birthday wish on a Facebook page rather then picking up the phone. Well...it is time to get back to the basics and invest in our relationships, connect with people, and start having conversations from the heart.

One of the reasons I love networking is because it brings people face to face. It's a time to connect and build relationships on a business and personal level. At one point, before advertising even existed, business was created solely by word of mouth; and it was

---

Seven Points of Impact

done because everyone knew everyone. Not much has changed today. We all still want to do business with people we know and like. What has changed is the amount of time we actually invest in getting to know the people with whom we are doing business.

So, I invite you to invest in your relationships...to open up and have heartfelt, honest conversations. Make the commitment to spend some time with the ones you like and the ones you love. You can create it all and have it look anyway you want. When we visualize what we want to create, we should remember it is the feeling that creates it. In the end, it really is the FEELING that you want to create which is important...not the THING itself.

About the Author

 As a chiropractor and a mother, Dr. Alison DiBarto's goal is to empower your family on its journey to be healthy. Originally from Ohio, and a graduate of Wittenberg University, Alison continued her education at Logan College of Chiropractic. She now resides in St. Louis, Missouri, where she specializes in pregnancy, pediatrics, grief resolution, nutrition and holistic healing modalities. Visit her website www.HealingHandsHealingLives.com for her complimentary healthy living newsletter and for future workshops and online workbooks.

Dr. Alison DiBarto can be reached at DrDiBarto@ HealingHandsHealingLives.com.

Surviving Suicide;
Growing Through the Grief and Guilt

By Alison DiBarto, D.C.

Deep down I always knew Patrick would never survive to see his niece born. He was one of my brothers, who struggled with a powerful drug addiction. Every time I saw him, I held him, hugged him, and kissed him until he pushed me away and called me an "idiot". I cherished each second, each phone call, always thinking to myself, "What if this is the last time I see him?"

The last time I did see him, I was nine months pregnant, visiting him in Ohio. My mom and I went to his friend's house where he was staying, because she had to confront him about stealing a family heirloom to sell for drugs. I was so distraught with the thought of him stealing from the family, I sat in the car. The last thing he said to me was that I looked gross, and I told him I loved him.

One week later, back in Missouri, I received a call from my brother Cameron. He told me Patrick was dead. He was only twenty years old. I was in denial. Patrick had a long history of drug abuse, overdoses, and close calls. I assumed this was another one of many overdoses and questioned Cameron about how he knew Patrick was dead. Did he overdose; was he breathing; how did he know? I refused to believe it when Cam told me Pat shot himself. I stood there numb, holding my belly and the precious baby growing inside me, while sobbing with the helplessness of the situation. Suicide was so definite, permanent, and violent. Patrick was gone, and there was nothing I could do to change that. Waves of guilt, confusion and anger came over me, yet I had to keep going for the sake of my unborn child.

The feelings we experience after such a violent death, as a survivor, are indescribable. Words such as pain, anger, grief, denial, hate, resentment, etc. do not even touch the surface. The only way to deal with these emotions is to be honest about your thoughts and talk with trusted friends and family around you. Most likely they are experiencing the same thoughts, and you can help each other. Mountains of research show the value of peer support groups in these and similar circumstances. Reach out and get the help you need. Monitor destructive behavior in yourself and family members. Drinking, drug use, and self-mutilation/cutting can escalate. I often felt the need to be with Patrick, to make sure he was okay even in death. I believed everything would be better if we could just be together.

I learned that experiencing feelings of suicide, cutting or other self-inflicting behaviors or thoughts often follow the loss from suicide. If you don't feel comfortable talking to family or friends, get professional help. Instead of hurting yourself, express your emotions by yelling, crying, sharing or even being silent. Don't judge yourself or the process you go through. Every person reacts differently, so let yourself and others grieve in their own right.

I held everything back and suffered silently. Personally, it has taken three years for me to openly talk about Patrick's death; I couldn't even talk to a counselor or close friends. But the pain never truly resolved; the emotions were simply suppressed. The more I meet others in this situation, I find we all agree that the pain never heals completely. Over a long period of time it lessens, but never truly dissolves. I found it comforting knowing that, when only one year had passed, the pain was the same as the day Cameron had called me; but I was not alone in having these feelings. Today the pain has lessened and continues to do so as I work on reconciling myself with Patrick's death.

The best advice we received from another family who lost a child was to journal stories of your loved one. Write down all the good, funny, sad, angry stories. Have friends and family who come to visit share their stories and memories. You will learn more than you ever wanted to about your loved one. Collect pictures and create a video. I surround myself with memories of a better, more peaceful time from our childhood pictures, items in a wood box that remind me of him, and scrapbook pages to help keep his memory alive for me in a healthy way.

Emotional help can come from support groups, religious centers, and also through physical healing. In my chiropractic practice many of my patients have been through similar situations. I agree when they explain how taking care of their own physical and emotional selves helps prevent the downfall into depression. Do one thing a day that makes you happy. It can be something small like listening to your favorite music, taking a long drive, getting a massage or a visit with animals, such as horses or dogs. Run your happy program as often as you can. When we keep our emotions locked up, our physical body takes the toll. An emotional stress can perpetuate a current physical symptom and even reignite an old injury. Some doctors use emotional healing techniques that help an individual cope with an experience, such as an accident or death. It is not necessary for the doctor to know of the situation; we can still treat the patient and help reduce the physical stress caused by emotional distress.

The gift of Patrick's death is that, in his tragedy, he saved lives. A young man heard about Patrick's death while in a rehabilitation clinic; and while his intention was to start using again and commit suicide after leaving the clinic, news of Patrick's death was a tragedy to him. He stopped using that day...the day he heard of Patrick's death.

Another friend left his two-year sobriety coin on Patrick's grave, which is now part of his headstone. Become an advocate for your loved one, and let his or her death give life to others. Be ever mindful that we have no control over their choices, yet we can use their stories to influence others to make better decisions.

Looking back, Patrick's suicide influenced my life in so many ways. I've searched to find the blessing amidst unspeakable tragedy. I lost a brother, but gained understanding, emotional maturity, strength and healing through this process. I learned to recognize the priority of my friends and family rather than meaningless busy work.

After Patrick's death my mom asked me, "If you knew you only had twenty years with someone, would you do everything differently?"

Of course, the answer is "yes"; but it is a good reminder that we need to live each day in our relationships as if they are the last moments we have with the people we love. When my daughter was born a few weeks after the funeral, I knew that she would always come first; and I would never let myself regret missing a minute with her.

Often we can have thoughts of regret and guilt that we should have done everything differently. I intuitively know I did my best, and Patrick's choices were beyond my ability to control. I must forgive myself for any shortcomings on my part, for all the things I did or did not do; and I must choose to go forward with greater purpose, for this will give my life greater meaning. At this point it is best to reach out to your spiritual side and get in contact with your priest, pastor or spiritual guides. Rest in the knowledge that "Spirit/God/Higher Power" has set a path in life for all of us, and we cannot control another person. Eliminate the blame and guilt.

Lastly, focus on the good stories about your loved one. Let his or her memory bring a smile to your life instead of pain. Always picture your loved one in a good place, whether it be heaven or on the beach. Trust and know that they are happy and loved, for surely God's grace and mercy far surpasses our own desires and intentions for our loved ones.

Point

5

Magnificent
Mental Mindset

About the Author

Lethia Owens is President/CEO of Lethia Owens International, Inc. She is a certified personal branding strategist, information-technology expert and business authority with more than 16 years of leadership experience and a strong track record of results. She is a highly-sought-after international speaker, coach, author and consultant to many Fortune 500 companies, churches and non-profit organizations.

Traveling from Dallas to Dubai, Lethia teaches people how to unearth their passions, realize their potential and embrace their phenomenal futures. As a messenger of hope, she helps others discover possibilities, develop strategies, plan purposefully and execute diligently. She uses her high value content, dynamic keynote presentations and engaging training programs to show others they, too, can achieve extraordinary results. Through the use of real-life stories and common sense strategies, she awakens the potential in clients and audiences to think, work and live powerfully. Her enthusiasm is contagious. She has the amazing ability to engage audiences in a way that allows them to envision new possibilities and eagerly anticipate future successes.

If you are looking for a dynamic speaker for your next event, contact Mrs. Owens today. She is guaranteed to inspire your audience to Think, Work & Live Powerfully!

Contact Lethia at: 636-244-5041 or Lethia@LethiaOwens.com

You are Bigger, More Powerful and More Valuable Than You Think

By Lethia Owens

In *The Lion King*, when Simba, the baby lion, doubts his power and potential, his father, Mufasa, says "Look. Look at who you are. Look at your reflection in the lake. You just forgot who you are!"

You also may have a case of mistaken identity and need to be reminded of who you really are. I am sure you have struggled with doubt—the wicked voice attempting to rob you of your greatness by convincing you that you are less than what you really are. It tells you that you are less capable than the power you possess.

The first step in transforming your life is accepting responsibility for where and who you are right now. Then you can effectively move towards the rewarding process of transitioning to where you really want to be. The biggest threat to your success is a mindset wired for failure...believing false information about yourself. It's time to discover the power of your true self, embrace your value and release your potential.

You're more amazing than you think...

You are bigger, more powerful and more valuable than you have been taught to believe. It's time to reprogram your thinking; discover the truth about who you are and what you're capable of achieving!

As children, we allow ourselves to dream freely about things we desire and results for which we hope. We let our minds and hearts soar to unbelievable heights envisioning ourselves doing amazing

---

things. We spend so much time visualizing the goal, we begin to believe the dream is real. Well, it's time to go back to that process of positive projection...and couple it with action.

Your life experiences are shaped by your thoughts; therefore, decide to think differently. One amazing truth about personal growth is that once you think differently, you act differently. In essence, you become what you think about. Did you know you actualize what you believe? Your brain doesn't know the truth from fiction; it believes everything you tell it.

Affirmations and visualizations are powerful tools you can use to help bring about transformational results. They are simply the truth...seen, spoken and experienced in advance. Affirmations are a powerful form of self-talk; positive statements that are framed in the present tense and are spoken as if true. Visualizations are similar except you use images instead of words. Use these tools to help you think differently so you begin to act differently. Your new positive actions will begin to create new positive results.

The biggest difference between successful people and unsuccessful people is not education, experience or resources, but the fact that successful people have learned to make habit and discipline their allies. Successful people work beyond pre-conceived barriers and narrow philosophies others set for them. They dream of, and work diligently towards, creating the success desired. In short, those who achieve lasting success have developed the mindset for it. They have the attitude that they have succeeded long before success actually catches up with them.

Developing a success-oriented mindset...
Having a mindset for success means you're unafraid of hard

work and commitment. Your purpose in life drives you towards success, and you are happy to be on the journey. A mindset for success enables you to see solutions and new avenues instead of problems and obstacles. Once your mind is set for success, you can give it your all; then you are sure to reach your goals. These principles can help:

- Optimism – choosing to believe that good is yet to come.
- Resilience – bouncing back from setbacks; persisting in the face of adversity
- Continuous Self-Renewal – working to bring about your best self

Your level of personal and professional success will be proportional to the way you perceive and react to challenges in your life. You must intentionally choose your mental outlook and decide how you will interpret and, more importantly, respond to the events of your life. This is one of your most powerful tools for generating success.

Optimism — Believing a greater good will prevail is essential for dealing with challenges life throws your way...

Each day, more than 50,000 thoughts pass through your mind, most of them unnoticed; unfortunately, research says 95 percent of your thoughts are negative. Would you like to learn how to make your thoughts serve to empower and motivate you instead of drain you? The key to developing a mind oriented towards optimism and success is understanding your beliefs shape your reality. If you have been taught to believe self-defeating, self-sabotaging ideas about yourself, these negative thoughts will manifest into defeat, causing you to act in a way that prevents you from achieving your desired success. On the other hand, choosing to use purposeful, passionate, positive and powerful affirmations about your value as a person and your potential and probability for success, you'll likely achieve the results you desire. Your perception is your reality. Henry Ford said, "If you think you can or you can't, you're right." Choose to believe you can.

Researcher, Dr. Martin Seligman, who works on learned helplessness and psychology at the University of Pennsylvania, reports that optimistic people get depressed less often, achieve more and enjoy significantly better health. Optimists tend to have a presumption of power and resilience programmed into their thought patterns. ***More importantly, Dr. Seligman's significant findings show optimism can be learned.***

Seligman's work corresponds with other authors, such as Carol S. Dweck, author of *Mindset: The New Psychology of Success*, which documents ways people with a "growth" mind-set believe they can improve themselves. In other words, optimists consistently outperform those with a "fixed" mindset who believe they have reached their maximum capabilities.

Dr. Toshihiko Maruta, researcher at the Mayo Clinic, reports that optimistic attitudes can dramatically affect a person's physical and mental functioning. A positive outlook and reaction to life can impact longevity and quality of life as a whole. In addition, a Johns Hopkins study showed that optimists outperform pessimists in all professional fields except one—law—primarily because they believe they are capable of effecting change and improving themselves.

Resilience—Bouncing Back from Life's Challenges...
The challenges of life are inevitable; your response to the challenges of life will determine your level of peace, success

and happiness. Your difficulty in making a comeback from life's setbacks may be a result of learned helplessness. Remember, you have a CHOICE in how you respond to the events of life. You are more powerful than the thoughts holding you back.

Here are five tools to help you develop resilience:

- **Visualization** – Imagine a big movie screen. On the screen, imagine your heart's desire. See it as if it is right in front of you. Now, step into the screen; see, feel, and hear what it would be like to be in the scene.

- **Affirmation** – Repetition is quite powerful to the subconscious mind. Affirmations draw on this power. The affirmations need to be in present tense, simple and positive, e.g., "I have the talent, knowledge and skills to excel at this task". Speak and repeat often.

- **Assumption** – Assume the characteristics you wish to embody. How would a calm person act? Embody those aspects.

- **Network** – Develop a support network with a few key people who can encourage you during difficult times.

- **Alternatives** – Have a backup plan, because things don't go as anticipated.

Finally—Make a commitment to Continuous Self Renewal...
You must take ownership for your success and begin the process of continuous self-renewal. No one will be more concerned with your personal and professional growth than you. Adopt a competitive spirit, and begin competing with your best self. Every dream and goal you have is counting on your commitment to this principle. Only you can give yourself permission to become your best by learning to think, work and live powerfully.

About the Author

Michelle Nelson, President and Founder of Back 2 Basics Marketing, LLC, has spent the past 21 years learning about consumer mindsets and the most effective advertising and marketing methods to reach them.

Michelle has owned Fortune 100 and 500 Marketing companies, including an event company, direct mail company, ad agency and was founder of the Outdoor Experience show. Michelle's expertise lies in increasing revenue through direct marketing to new and existing customers, developing key relationships, and creative marketing through web design, collateral materials and direct marketing efforts. Through her years of experience, Michelle has learned that customers do in fact, come first.

In 2007, Michelle Nelson dreamed of owning her own marketing company again. Nelson visited the St. Louis area frequently and after doing extensive research on local businesses she quickly realized something... there was not a marketing communications company that tailored its services to both small and large businesses in the areas of marketing. After much thought, Nelson was ready to make a change and went back to her hometown of Peoria, IL, packed up her son, dog and cat, and settled in St. Charles County. That year Back 2 Basics Marketing, LLC was founded by Nelson with less than $300.00.

By creating Back 2 Basics Marketing, LLC, Michelle was out to prove the best way to gain customer trust and return business. Her mission was to deliver an exceptional product, at a fair price and timely manner. Back 2 Basics Marketing, LLC is dedicated to delivering successful marketing strategies for businesses without the process, layers and 3-hour meetings. Nelson offers her clientele full service marketing, specializing in advertising, public relations, web and graphic design and as well as event coordination. Today, Back 2 Basics Marketing, LLC has over 150 clients nationwide with offices in St. Louis, Missouri and Denver, Colorado.

In addition to her marketing expertise, Michelle is an award winning speaker. She has presented key note speeches, workshops and seminars all across the United States. Topics discussed include:

- Successful marketing techniques that will work in a weak economy.
- Ways to utilize current marketing budgets
- Effective direct marketing efforts
- Public Relations and Event Management tools
- Blogs
- Social Networking
- User generated content
- Internet Marketing
- Effectively using Trade and Barter Exchanges

Michelle's optimistic attitude is reflected in every service that she provides her customers. One thing you will quickly learn about Michelle Nelson is that she is always smiling. She is a member of the eWomenNetwork Greater St. Louis Metropolitan chapter, O'Fallon Chamber of Commerce and Wentzville Chamber of Commerce in Missouri.

Connect with Michelle & the Back 2 Basics Staff at:
www. Back2BasicsMarketing.com

Don't Let Your Dreams Die

By Michelle Nelson

Have you ever just woken up from a dead sleep, looked around your bedroom, and realized that your life sucks? How about being divorced twice and left with a broken heart? Broke and eating spaghetti every day? What about being trapped in a dead-end job in small-town, USA??

Well, that would be me on July 18, 2007. I woke before the sun, at 4:00 a.m. on a Saturday morning, looked around my bedroom, stared at the walls, and said out loud, "Is this my life? This cannot be my life; I need a do over!"

I put the pillow over my head and attempted to go back to sleep. That didn't work. I got up and went to McDonalds for my usual Egg McMuffin and coffee, something I shouldn't have done, considering I was strapped for cash, as usual. I just sat in my dining room area, eating my "expensive" breakfast, surveying the surroundings, and said, "I am ready to make a change."

You see, at that point in time, I was $200,000 in debt; and I was always $100 away from being overdrawn on my accounts. The reality of my financial situation was gut-wrenching! In addition, I worked for a company with a boss who didn't see eye to eye with me on anything, except the fact that we disliked each other very much. Facing the harsh reality of that situation, I decided bravery and boldness were the order of the day. After getting out of the shower, almost on autopilot, I got dressed. With my hair still wet,

I slipped on my flip flops and jeans that had seen better days, and went into the office, knowing my boss would be there working on a Saturday morning.

With the promise of new-found freedom beaconing me, I entered her office without hesitation. Vowing to be honest, I sat down and said, "Let's face it, you don't like me just as much as I don't like you. If I stay and continue working for you, I am going to turn into you; and I don't like the person you have become."

It didn't take long for her to call HR, then security; and I was escorted out. I will never forget what the HR director said to me, smiling, as she led me to the door, "Mitzy, you are going to be okay; you are going to be just fine." It was as if she knew. I held on to those words for the next year very closely.

I drove home; and by that point, my son, Ian, was out of bed. "Where have you been?" he wanted to know.

I said, "I quit my job!"

You can imagine his surprise! "What?" he stammered in disbelief.

My heart swelled with compassion, as I repeated my words and offered an explanation. "I quit my job, Ian. You know, we are always close to being penniless. This house needs more repairs than I can manage; I hate what I do, and I want to experience living somewhere larger than this small town. But I will not move us, if you don't want to move."

Ian was my second confirmation that I needed to follow my intuition. He said, "Mom, I agree. If we don't eventually have to struggle like we do right now, and it would be a better life for us, then we need to move." In that moment, I loved him more than words could ever express.

The third confirmation came when, after sending out a mass email, my house rented in less than an hour!

Then I thought, "WOW, what do I do now? Now I am not going to have a place to live, I have no job, and no money." It was then I began weighing my options. I had lived in St. Louis when I was in college and had since visited a friend who lived in O'Fallon, Missouri. After "surveying" the area, I started thinking St. Louis just might be a great place to start another ad agency. "But how?", I thought. I had no assets to my name, except the $1,000 in rent money I had just gotten, which needed to go to the mortgage.

I did have a wonderful boyfriend who had said he would move with us; and I thought he would be with me the rest of my life. At least we wouldn't be totally alone! He said eventually he would move there. So with that premise, we started packing. A week later, that house was completely empty; and Ian, the dog, the cat, and I were in the SUV driving to St Louis.

I will never forget all of our family and friends standing on the side road, by our home, waving at us in the rear view mirror. I looked over at Ian, and he was crying. Then I started to cry, which lasted all the way to St. Louis.

Fast forward...St. Louis. We got unpacked and started settling in. We were miserable! We knew no one! Ian had to start a new school! We had no money! We were eating lunch meat sandwiches for breakfast, lunch, and dinner; and if it wasn't that, it was spaghetti! Everywhere I went people asked me what high school I went to! (If you are reading this and wondering why people asked me that—it's a St. Louis thing.) I just believed they thought I was too young to be in business!

Unfortunately, St. Louis wasn't the immediate answer to our dreams. At one point, I had less than $300 to my name. One particular day, when Ian returned home from school, I had to be honest with him. "I have sold everything I can sell; and we have no money, Ian."

I had no job, no freelance work, no nothing! On top of that, the boyfriend I thought would be in my life forever couldn't fathom uprooting his own life to join mine. He left our relationship without even having a conversation with me. On a road trip home, he just didn't show up; and I have never seen him since.

So there we were one day, Ian and I, alone and friendless on one of our tight-budgeted grocery store runs. Having nothing much in the house to eat, I told Ian all we could afford were eggs, spaghetti and simple things that were long sustaining. Spontaneously, tears began to well up; and I started to cry. Through my tears, I asked Ian, "What have I done moving us here? We know no one. I took you away from the home you always knew, friends, family that was close in distance..."

I will never forget him looking up at me and saying, at age 13, "Buck up, Mom. You did the right thing moving us here. You are good at what you do, now start doing it!"

Just like that, my own son was giving me advice. I suddenly felt like the 13 year old that he was. There was no denying this experience had formed a deep and abiding love between us.

Wiping the tears away, we continued on our shopping mission. As we headed down one of the aisles, suddenly I was tapped on the shoulder by a stranger asking if I could help with a wine display. I thought it was a bit weird...but okay. After helping the gentleman, he asked, "What do you do for a living?" I responded with, "What do you need done?"

Through that connection, I soon had my first client. At the time, I didn't have a name for my company. One day, not long after our grocery store experience, I was sitting with Ian discussing our current status. "Our life is Back 2 the Basics", I recall telling him. In that moment, the inspiration came to me.

From that simple thought, the company name and mission were born; and really, that's what I want to do for companies...take them Back 2 the Basics. I want to remind them what made them go into business in the first place and take their marketing back 2 the basics...back to their inspiration!

In the beginning, I worked three jobs, including running the company. I did that for a year and half, until I was completely debt free. Ian and I still ate spaghetti, but only when we wanted to. On my birthday, June 30, 2008, I launched the business full time—Back 2 Basics Marketing, LLC. Today we have 200 clients nationwide, along with eight full-time team members. We are getting ready to franchise Back 2 Basics Marketing, LLC, by October, 2010; and soon a franchise will be available near you.

My goal in life is to help anyone who has ever thought about having his or her own ad agency. I want to teach people everything I know, including all of the mistakes I made, in order to help that person avoid those same pitfalls, and end up with the most successful business possible.

If you are reading my story, I beg you to take a chance with your life. I was 36 years old at the start of my great adventure, and I am so glad I took the chance. I am glad I didn't listen to anyone who doubted me or I would still be back in my hometown, broke, restless, and wondering what my life's purpose was supposed to be. I dared to keep dreaming when there were many who had given up on me. Don't let other people talk you out of your dreams! Take the chance! Your true friends will always be with you, no matter what...and more will show up. If I have inspired just one person with my story, it is worth the telling.

As my son said to me, "Buck up, and just do it!"

About the Authors

 Dawn and Drew Ferguson are the founders of Ferguson and Associates Hypnotherapy. Their goal is to empower their clients with a proven process that moves them from struggle to success rapidly. Over the years, they have expanded their business to serve a host of local, regional and international clients either in person, by phone or via the internet. From the States to Europe, your success is just one call away!

There is power in defining your own belief system. "You will be it when you believe it" is an assurance you can rely on. If you desire to learn more about self-hypnosis, Dawn and Drew conduct regular sessions and webinars that may help you gain the knowledge you seek and the changes you desire.

Additional information and tools are available to you on their website. They invite you to claim your F-R-E-E mini e-book "3 Secrets to Your Success and 3 Mistakes that Lead to Struggle" visit www.fergusonhypnotherapy.com

You Will Be It When You Believe It

By Dawn & Drew Ferguson

The Tooth Fairy, the Easter Bunny, Santa Claus, even the Boogeyman who hid under the bed, are all childhood beliefs that we all chose to let go of so we could make room for more "adult" beliefs...except for the Boogeyman. Things that go bump in the night can still get to us. But what if there are still "scary" beliefs hanging around in the basement of our minds? What if there are other beliefs that are holding us back???

First, let's start with...what is a belief? A belief is a thought that we have accepted as reality, whether it is the truth or not. One famous belief that demonstrates the power of misconceptions: the earth is flat, and the sun revolves around it. It is said that 80% of our beliefs are accepted by age 8 and a full 90% by age 13. We learned our beliefs through repetition..."you are so stupid" or "you did great on that"... and times of intense emotion like getting an "A" and our big brother telling us it was just "dumb luck". Our families may have encouraged our belief in the Tooth Fairy because it brought a touch of magic and whimsy to our lives. Yet, what else might they have encouraged us to believe without realizing it; "money does not grow on trees" or "only girls (or boys) can do that", maybe "you look just like your Aunt Sara" (who had the biggest hips and largest back side in the whole family). Yes, just what did our first families teach us?

So, how do you know when you have a belief that is holding you back? This is the easy part; look at your results in any area of your life. From how much you weigh to the amount of money you make, the relationships you form, the career you pick, even your spiritual path is determined by your beliefs. This is not a blame game though; it is time to stop the struggle. Do you have a goal that you have tried to achieve, yet it seems out of your grasp? Self sabotage? Or maybe you actually achieve the goal but then lose it? If you have repeatedly struggled with achieving and maintaining a goal, you may have a negative belief that is holding you back.

Why can't you just make the decision to change that area of your life by changing your actions or how you think? This results in just treating the symptoms and never getting to the cause. Imagine that you have a stomach ache. There might be multiple causes; intolerance for certain foods, maybe a medical condition that needs to be addressed. Without knowing the true cause, you repeatedly take antacids, never really feeling healthy; always a bit down in your energy, not knowing when the next attack of pain may occur. Your full potential of being vibrant and alive never materializes, because you are always dealing with the warning signs, but never the cause.

Looking at your lack luster results, you can discover that you have a challenge with a belief. Discovering what that belief is can take a bit of work. This is because your beliefs are not readily apparent on the surface...also known as the conscious mind. Your conscious mind is the part of you that rationalizes, justifies and analyzes. This is where you make deliberate, intentional decisions based on either achieving pleasure or avoiding pain. Since old beliefs can equal pain, your conscious mind can keep them suppressed and repressed. This is why you treat symptoms, not causes. Since the conscious mind is limited in its scope, it only accounts for 10-20% of your potential, power and success.

Your subconscious mind holds the remaining 80-90% of your life's achievement because of its many functions. It runs all of your habits and patterns, is the storehouse for all of your memories, and it holds all of your beliefs. The challenge is that it recalls these beliefs from the maturity level of when you first formed that belief. To further the challenge, it then runs the habits and patterns to support that belief.

Let's say you learned at age 8 (by watching your father) that you had to work long and hard to get ahead, and a belief was formed. Now, it's decades later for you and financial success is much easier than it was for your father, yet you feel "undeserving" because you have not worked "hard enough" for it. You may self sabotage by over spending or even hold yourself back from further success because of the belief, "work long and hard". That younger 8 year old you is running your financial program. To truly transform, you will need to make a conscious decision to release what was believed at 8 and then reinforce it by using the rules of your subconscious mind.

Rule One: The subconscious will not tolerate a void. Whatever belief, thought, emotion and/or coping behavior you wish to remove must be replaced with an alternative pattern. Either you consciously choose the replacement or your subconscious will make that decision for you. Beware of choosing by default, the subconscious always chooses habits based on pain avoidance. These show up as tension-relieving activities instead of goal achieving (think of a smoker who decides to quit and winds up over-eating). Make a conscious decision what new habits will replace the old.

Rule Two: Have a clear, definite end result in mind. The subconscious does not judge that you meant to make 100k this year when you decided to work with prosperity. It can find a nickel on the floor and feel more prosperous, so choose clear, compelling and conceivable conclusions.

Rule Three: Work with one area of your life at one time. Either your; health, wealth, career, relationships or spirituality. Although your subconscious mind can do many activities at once (right now it is handling your breathing, heart rate, digestion and thinking about options for dinner), your conscious mind is only adept at doing one thing at a time. You will need the cooperation of your conscious mind to carry out the actions to support your new belief. Allow it the time to achieve your Success. Just how long will that take? It takes 3 days to let go of a habit, 21 days to form its replacement, and 91 days to experience full results.

Rule Four: When you want to make changes in your subconscious, the best way is to communicate directly with your subconscious. This is accomplished through what is known as an Alpha brain wave state; another name: Hypnosis. Just a light, relaxed state, comparable to day dreaming or meditating, is a deep enough Alpha (Hypnotic) state to make the changes you desire. Although we do not wish to over-simplify, self hypnosis is possible with some simple techniques.

To begin, you will need a quiet environment, free of distractions. After you have entered a light, relaxed state, do the following; Go back to the last time you experienced _____ (struggle). Allow yourself to experience the challenge for just a moment. Next, ask your mind to go back to the time when your mind first decided that this should be a struggle. What was happening at that time that helped you decide this should be a struggle? What belief did you develop because of this?

Assure yourself that you have been doing the best you could with what you have learned. Now it is time for that younger you to experience joy in life and the older, wiser part of you to step forward with your new belief. Feel yourself experiencing empowerment because of this new belief; see yourself taking the actions to support this new belief. Experience the improvement in your life now that this belief is a habit for you. Give yourself permission to be the best you possibly can be in this area. See it, feel it, hear it, as if your Success has already happened. Repeat this exercise until you feel this new belief becoming a part of you.

Rule Five: Take at least one action every day to support your new belief. It takes anywhere from 21 to 91 days before your actions become automatic. Yet, by investing just a few weeks into your Success, how much better will your life be than it is now?

Your beliefs are the blueprints upon which you build your life. If the blueprint is sound, so is your success. If the blueprint is flawed, so are your results. Which do you choose? You will be it when you believe it.

Additional information and tools are available when you visit: www.fergusonhypnotherapy.com

About the Author

ERIN MURPHY, CPC, SVH – Serenity Life Coach. As an internationally-known Coach and Master Practitioner and Teacher of Serenity Vibration Healing®, Erin has been studying and personally implementing the philosophies behind personal development, self-discovery, psychology, metaphysics, quantum physics, spirituality and various energy healing modalities for over a decade.

- **As a Life Coach** who specializes in assisting women to find a sense of peace and purpose within their lives, Erin empowers them to take a closer look at the boxes they've created around themselves, redefine limiting parameters, and step into the life they are meant to live.

- **As a Master Practitioner and Teacher of Serenity Vibration Healing®**, she's helped hundreds of clients and students quiet their negative mind chatter and neutralize the drama, trauma and imbalance in their lives so they can create the space to discover their inner power and true desires.

- **As a Wife, Mother and Business Owner,** she understands how easy it is for women to lose a sense of their own personal identity while taking care of life's endless list of daily responsibilities. She knows that the difference between a life full of stress and overwhelm and one full of serenity revolves around a women's ability to know, love and appreciate herself.

For "Life Coaching with a Twist"™, contact Erin at: www.newrealmsofpossibility.com.

Be SELFish

By Erin Murphy, CPC, SVH

In our society, we have been conditioned to put others before ourselves, because putting ourselves first means we're selfish. Talking about our personal accomplishments or strengths is considered arrogant; it is only appropriate to say wonderful things about others. We are also unknowingly taught to be "yes-women" (or "yes-men"); saying no or setting boundaries means we're not nice or good people.

Following these norms blindly promotes a feeling of being a "good" person, yet the deeper feelings are often overwhelm, guilt, self-denial and confusion. Being a "good" person has turned us into people pleasers who care too much about what others think, who struggle to say "no" and rarely make SELF a priority. If being a "good" person doesn't feel good to you, shouldn't that be a sign something's amiss?

With any new awareness or realization that something isn't working for you comes the ability to create a new plan. To make "good" feel good, start by going within and give your SELF permission to be SELFish. Being SELFish simply means paying attention to and loving SELF. SELFish-ness is necessary to live a balanced, joyful life. You will never find the peace and fulfillment you desire in life if SELF is never on your agenda.

There are many steps on the journey to being SELFish. In this chapter, we're going to address the top four qualities and characteristics that embody a SELFish woman.

Four Qualities of a SELFish Woman:

- Saying "No" Without Guilt
- Making SELF a Priority
- Not Caring What Others Think
- Tooting Your Own Horn

Saying "No" Without Guilt

To embody SELFish, it is important to be able to say "no" without feeling guilty. Most people say "yes" because they would rather sacrifice their time and energy than cause conflict or experience feelings of guilt. We've all said "yes" to someone knowing our true desire was to say "no". Saying "yes" when we want to say "no" causes a disconnect between our words and our intentions, which can lead to upset, overwhelm and stress. It's okay to say "no". By saying "no", you're not only being true to your SELF, but you're also respecting everyone involved.

In order to say "no" without the guilt, you'll want know what is important to you and if what is being requested fits into those parameters. Make sure you're choosing to spend your time, energy and effort on the things that matter most to you. It is also important to stop being so nice. If you say "yes" just to be nice, chances are you'll follow through half-heartedly or resent doing what you agreed to do. People can tell when your words and thoughts don't match your actions. Also understand that saying "no" means nothing more than saying "no". You are simply saying "no" to the request, not rejecting the person.

SELFish Action Steps:

- Clarify what your highest priorities are.

- Practice saying "no" to requests that are not in alignment with your highest priorities. Saying "no" to something that you don't really want to do or feel obligated to do is like saying "yes" to your SELF.

Making Self a Priority

We have responsibilities galore and to-do lists that never end, yet a SELFish woman also guiltlessly includes herself in her list of daily activities.

Many women struggle to find where "me time" fits into their schedule, and they feel overwhelmed by the volume of things they need to accomplish each day. To "find" time, we typically cut out our personal activities or we long ago stopped planning time for our SELF. We buy into the illusion that sacrificing SELF is the only way to get everything done.

What is the cost of such SELF sacrifice? We feel drained, unhappy, unmotivated, unfulfilled, unclear and inefficient in our lives. SELF sacrifice simply doesn't work. We need time for SELF to refuel, re-energize, and recharge our batteries for what tomorrow brings. As a result, we're more efficient in the tasks we take on and clearer about the choices we face each day. Making time for SELF is a priority; and to reframe how we see "me-time", we typically need to schedule it.

SELFish Action Steps:

- Schedule time for you. Get out your calendar, and schedule it as an appointment to do something for you—meditate, exercise, read a book, get a massage, eat healthy—anything you find fun or enjoyable that is just for you. By the way, doing something for someone else because you enjoy it doesn't count!

Not Caring What Others Think

The only way to truly become SELFish is to stop caring what others think about you, stop letting their opinions have more value than your own, and start trusting your SELF!

Have you ever avoided doing something because of what others may think? Have you ever started second guessing or doubting yourself because someone else thought it would work better another way? The opinions of others have a tendency to trump our own and often make us second guess what we think we think. We automatically believe the other person knows more than we do. We even fear the potential conflict if we voice our point of view.

It is okay to not agree with what your best friend, mother or husband/wife thinks. When we constantly conform, we inadvertently hand over the reins of our life to the opinions (or potential opinions) of others and shut down our ability to tune into our intuition. It is time to get back in the driver's seat and find the balance between conforming to the opinions of others and taking those opinions into consideration as part of our own decision making process.

SELFish Action Steps:

- Be clear about what you think/feel/believe and why. When you become grounded in your opinion, you can consider the opinions of others without doubting yourself. Sometimes both points of view will mesh; sometimes they won't.

Tooting Your Own Horn

In becoming SELFish, we become our own biggest cheerleader, acknowledge our greatness and our strengths, and learn how to pat ourselves on the back.

As women, we have a tendency to look outside ourselves for love, acceptance and a sense that our lives are moving in the right direction. It is totally acceptable to tell someone else that they're great at something. Yet if we say we're great at something, we may be perceived as conceited. We even deny compliments in an effort to not look arrogant or full of ourselves.

What is this doing to our sense of SELF, our SELF-esteem?

Every time we look outside ourselves or we deny a compliment, we're adding another layer of "fog" to the already unclear definition of who we are. Who we are then becomes more difficult to find, define or discover. Most women struggle with the question of who they are because of their inability to be SELFish. If you're one of them, learning to toot your own horn is a step toward that clarification you desire.

SELFish Action Steps:

- Define one thing you're great at every day. Write it down for future reference, and tell someone else what you've discovered about you.

Please remember, you don't have to do it alone! There are New Realms of Possibilities available...www.newrealmsofpossibility.com

---

About the Author

 Paige Russell; M. Ed – Human Services, Bachelor's Psychology & Criminology, and Certified Hypnotist. Paige is a Life & Success Coach and Hypnotist who prefers to be known as the "Juicy Life-Stylist & Solutionist". She believes in the phenomenal and powerful ability of your mind and partners with you to help YOU achieve transformational success!

Paige can be your team-mate...propelling you to a more fulfilling and abundant future!

Connect with Paige at: www.Dragonfly-Elementals.com

Review – Release – Relearn

By Paige Russell

I am not a **<u>Stupid Bitch</u>**... or... I am **<u>NOT</u>** a stupid bitch! One underlined word in a sentence can completely change a thought or a belief. One point of emphasis in our memory patterns can signify a belief prevalent for a person. Consider how one careless, hurtful comment can linger for years to come. Those memories, those thoughts, were some of my challenges.

By the time I turned 40, I had an impressive resume of career accomplishments. I had also been through two marriages, experienced verbal, physical and sexual abuse by people who truly loved me, buried both parents, overcome a dependency on prescription sleeping pills, and wrestled with self-injury and depression. I was able to inspire and motivate others in their lives, but never could seem to locate that magic key to transform my own life. It took 40 years of life lessons to understand that I had the power to embrace a new mental mindset to transform my life.

The phenomenal Maya Angelou once said, "Take a day to heal from the lies you've told yourself and that have been told to you." It is time to realize how liberating and life-changing it is to become what you believe, because your world is exactly what you think. Your day starts now.

Fast forward to the here and now—I am what I am, full speed ahead, ovaries to the wall, baby! I'm rip-roaring, rarin' to go; ready to jump in there and savor being alive! I have learned that as life unfolds, we give back, pay it forward, and make a difference in this existence. Every single person reading this book has his or her own self-defeating, negative self-talk and can relate to having an "inner monologue of pooper-doopers". Every person reading this chapter has a valuable story worth listening to and learning from. What are your stories?

The stories that we hold in our minds are incredibly intense and affect us on a level of the highest magnitude. These stories hold great power over us and feed into the belief systems that run our lives. Beliefs are evidence-based, and it can be estimated that over 80% of the beliefs that you carry around with you today were formed and accepted by the time you were 8 years old. Over 90% of the beliefs you lug around were formed and accepted by the time you were 13 years old. Who most likely had the primary influence on forming these beliefs? So often it was those who were in authority at the time or the people with whom you spent the most time. So shall we blame the parent, blame the grade school bully, blame the mean teacher, and throw ourselves a most remarkable Pity Party? Admittedly, many of us have kicked up our heels at such parties, playing the blame game; but if you want to change your life, you have to come back to looking at the mental clutter of outdated beliefs that hurt you.

The whole idea isn't to remain stuck in the "WHY" mode of the past. Instead, we look at the "WHAT" and the "HOW": What was going on? Review the reality of what happened. What do you feel and what do you know about what happened? How can you change how you feel about this? How can you learn from it and take the lesson with you, but leave behind the attachment to the event and the attachment to the beliefs that hurt you? Review ~ Release ~ Relearn!

How can you overcome obstacles, get through the difficult times and survive in this day and age? You roll up your sleeves; you start dealing with it and embrace being progressive, not regressive. You look at the areas in your life that are stressful and hurtful. You review the things in your life that are not working and have not been working for years; you hone in on areas and issues where it's been like trying to nail JELLO to a tree! Then you take some precious time for yourself and start distilling it down to determine what one significant BELIEF you currently carry around and cling to. What is the one most powerful belief that you have been holding onto and have allowed to completely run your life—your eating habits, your relationships, your self-esteem? What belief could stand to be reviewed, released, and relearned? Such beliefs can hold a person hostage and trap one in a perpetual state of emotional blackmail. When you read the following, put a mental checkmark by the beliefs that a part of your mind has bought into in the past or still believes right here, right now:

You are stupid. You are lazy...boring...fat...ugly. You are just like your mother. No one will ever love you. You can't do that. I wish you had never been born. Keeping you was a mistake. You are the only one who can take care of everything. You are a stupid bitch. You're always wrong. You are nothing without a husband. Who would ever want someone like you? You always screw up. You'll never make it on your own. You are not worthy. You are _____.

Do any of these beliefs sound familiar? Did your mind fill in the blank with yet one more negative and hurtful belief? If so, then what NEW BELIEFS could you possibly absorb and own, after reviewing and releasing those that have been holding you down?

What new truisms can your powerful mind begin to explore, and how do you go about finding them?

Seek out, discover, and surround yourself with people who inspire and challenge you. Uncover and approach those who have the talent, training and knowledge on a wide variety of things that can completely rock and change your world. If you change your mind, your life will follow! If this is not the life you ordered... then review, release, and relearn. Give your powerful mind the tools it needs to create your own true life and reality, on your terms. Be prepared to hit it hard, scream at the top of your lungs, cry until you are drier than bone; that's part of the reviewing and releasing. But then as you relearn, be prepared to laugh uproariously, dance like a crazy-ass nut-ball, and accept all the love, expertise, wisdom, and assistance that are out there along the way. Life IS good. We are all connected. You are worthy. You are radiant; you have talents and abilities that are meant to shine. Nothing and no one can hold you back.

A painting hangs on my office wall, and it says, "Once you start to listen, everything will become clear; and once you decide to fly, your wings will never stop moving" by Heather Handler of Myklo Designs. It is time to discover and embrace some really wonderful truisms that will help you become what you believe, because your world is exactly what you think—and you are totally worth that!

•••••••••

Are you looking to spruce up your personal life by reclaiming your self-confidence, better manage stress, cease smoking, reduce and maintain your weight, improve your body image, seek healthier lifestyle choices or just improve your relationships with partners, spouses, and children? Have you hit a professional and career "plateau" that has you seeking ways to better achieve goals, gain confidence, embrace public speaking, or move forward and up the career ladder? Are you an athlete or a performing artist who needs to fine-tune your concentration levels and optimize your performance? Have you been suffering with feelings of sadness, grief, or sleeplessness? Are you experiencing 'Money Angst' or 'Career Anxiety'? Or are you simply tired of feeling listless, uninspired, and "beaten-down" by life?

Focusing on you at the Physical, Emotional, and Mental level, Paige can utilize many different techniques (hypnosis, meditation, guided visualizations, and even some good old-fashioned "Drag your tookus out of bed and into Life" actions) to help you zap those obstacles, crunch outdated and ineffective habits, and bring about outstanding results and changes in your life. Paige can be your team-mate...propelling you to a more fulfilling and abundant future!

Connect with Paige at: www.Dragonfly-Elementals.com

About the Author

 Rev. Deborah "Russ" Russell has been a teacher of Mindfulness-Based Stress Reduction for more than ten years and a daily meditation practitioner for more than twenty years. She is a dispute resolution mediator for the City of Albuquerque, a volunteer chaplain for University of New Mexico Hospital and an Integral Life Coach in private practice. Russell and her husband, Rev. Joe Galewsky, are the resident priests of Desert Mirror Zendo and Guest House in Albuquerque, NM.

To find out more about how meditation and other mindfulness practices can help you, contact Rev. Russell about individual or group coaching at www.desertmirror.org

<u>A</u>ttention and <u>I</u>ntention

By Rev. Deborah "Russ" Russell

Being happy by covering over life's sorrows—impermanence and loss—is not a good way to be happy, because those things have a way of catching up to you.

– Norman Fischer, Zen teacher and poet

Let's face facts: Life doesn't always conform to our preferences. Sometimes things don't go the way we want them to. Sometimes they go exactly the way we don't want them to. Even when things are really going our way, just under that great "Ahhhh, now this is what I'm talkin' about!" feeling, there's always a hint of anxiety over the possibility that something will change. It always does— and that lovely "Ahhhh" feeling will fade into a memory. So we keep working hard to find and hang onto what we think will bring pleasure; and we do our best to avoid what we think will cause pain, either physical or emotional. It's an endless effort to control life (which is inherently uncontrollable); and the strain of it all produces a kind of ongoing, low-level (or sometimes pretty high-level) stress.

In this endless, stressful effort to control life, keeping a firmly fixed mind "set" seems sensible, especially in the North American "failure is not an option" culture. But setting your mind in a fixed way in any direction is likely to produce resistance and maybe even movement in the opposite direction. In fact, one of the most fundamental facts we know about our world is Newton's Third Law: "For every action, there is an equal and opposite reaction." And you've probably heard the saying of former 1970s feminist activist, Sonia Johnson: "What we resist persists."

So if having a firmly fixed mindset isn't really such a skillful approach, and if constantly moving toward pleasure and away from pain actually produces stress, what might be a better way to try to live? This is a basic question that human beings have been asking themselves and each other for centuries.

About 2,500 years ago, a nobleman named Siddhartha Gautama set out to answer some of these basic questions for himself. He spent quite a few years pursuing his quest, and he eventually had some major insights about how we cause ourselves stress and how we can eliminate that self-induced stress.

More recently, in the 1970s and 80s, some of the simple techniques taught by the Buddha (The Awakened One, as Siddhartha Gautama came to be known) were adapted for use in secular, western cultures. Since then, hundreds of thousands of Americans have learned to reduce their stress levels and maintain a more flexible, peaceful mental state by focusing their attention and intention through the practice of mindfulness.

What is Mindfulness?
For our purposes, mindfulness can be thought of as a set of conscious intentions and simple, practical techniques that can help us be more fully aware of the present moment. Taking a mindful approach to life helps us to see more clearly whatever is happening right now and to acknowledge things as they are, without judging the current reality or needing to change it. Having a committed mindfulness practice can be a way to develop a friendlier and more accepting relationship with yourself and your own life. Living from within this greater self-awareness and self-acceptance just naturally produces more

compassion for the other individuals, institutions and situations we find in our lives.

That sounds good. I want to feel more self-acceptance and compassion. But you said mindfulness was a set of intentions and techniques. Give me some examples.

The most common form of mindfulness practice is probably daily meditation, which is currently practiced by millions of people around the world; and more people are taking it up all the time. Here in the U.S., physicians prescribe mindfulness training for patients with all kinds of chronic medical conditions; and clinical research shows that taking up mindfulness practices for even just eight weeks can produce significant reductions in people's symptoms.

Now, you may think that meditation is too exotic or too hard for ordinary people with busy lives to really practice seriously. But it's not. It's actually quite simple. An experienced mindfulness teacher could show you the basics of seated meditation in about five minutes; and there are lots of other simple mindfulness practices that could also be adapted to fit neatly into your regular life, just as it is right now. In fact, it's precisely because the practices are so simple and adaptable that they're so powerful and potentially transformative.

Doesn't meditation require chanting some kind of weird mantra or somehow emptying my busy mind while sitting in some weird, pretzel-like position?

There are many different varieties of meditation; some involve the use of mantras and some do not. Many people who practice meditation do sit in some kind of cross-legged position, but it is not necessary to sit on the floor in order to meditate. You can sit in your favorite chair, on the couch or at your desk in your office. You can even meditate while walking or lying down. The point of mindfulness meditation isn't really to empty your mind; it's to notice and be fully present with whatever is happening right now—which might often include having a busy, chattering mind.

Well, so how do I learn to meditate?

It's best to get some instruction from someone who is well-qualified to teach meditation—maybe someone associated with a Zen, Insight or Shambhala meditation program—or from your local hospital's Mindfulness-Based Stress Reduction program. On the other hand, I first read about meditation in books, and I practiced on my own for three years before ever attending my first in-person instruction. The important thing is to just try to begin. If curiosity about your own life captures your interest, you can almost certainly find good instruction somewhere in your area. (There are also lots of good meditation teachers who offer free, guided meditation online.)

For right now, just sit comfortably in a chair, with both feet flat on the floor, and begin to feel your body's contact with all the places where the chair and the floor are supporting you. Notice the areas of contact beneath your feet, under your legs and rear end, maybe under your arms, etc. Formulate the intention to focus on your breathing as much as possible for five minutes and to not judge yourself when you find your mind wandering.

Now bring your attention to your breathing. Feel the air entering your nostrils and moving back through your throat and down into your lungs. Feel the chest and belly rising on the in-breath and falling back on the out-breath. Try to ride each breath like a wave, all the way in and all the way out. Perhaps you will notice that your breaths are not all exactly alike.

When you eventually notice that your thoughts have taken you away from the breath, as they inevitably will, just return to the breath—without judgment—over and over again. This is meditation. You're doing it. Now, that wasn't so hard, was it?

> "As we all know, we can think about changing our emotional lives for a thousand years and nothing will change. But as soon as we sit and breathe, opening the field of awareness somatically, we have a different—and wiser—access to what is within us."
>
> – Norman Fischer, Founder of EverydayZen.org

Suggested Reading:

Full Catastrophe Living, by Jon Kabat-Zinn

A Mindfulness-Based Stress Reduction Workbook, by Bob Stahl & Elisha Goldstein

The Miracle of Mindfulness, by Thich Nhat Hanh

Connect with the Author:

To find out more about how meditation and other mindfulness practices can help you, contact Rev. Russell about individual or group coaching at www.desertmirror.org

About the Author

Cathy Sexton has been a productivity strategist and coach since 2003. Cathy uses her passion and empathetic nature to help people live healthy, productive lives! She knows the health risks of being a workaholic; she has lived it. Her purpose in life is to provide coaching, teaching, and tools to people who are hungry to spend more time with family, enjoy their careers while living a less stressed and more carefree life.

Cathy owns and operates The Productivity Experts, offering organizing and productivity skills training to business leaders and work groups. The Productivity Experts help individuals ignite their performance. As more business professionals struggle with the daily pressures of endless to-do's and less time to do them, The Productivity Experts help their clients discover their **natural productivity style** so they can work smarter, not harder.

For a free productivity assessment, visit:
www.TheProductivityExpers.com
or Cathy@TheProductivityExperts.com

I Dream of an Organized Life, But....

By Cathy Sexton

Are you one of the millions of people who commonly says, "If only I had more time..." or " If only I were more organized..."; "There is no way I can get all this done" or "I need to get organized, but I don't know where to start"? With all we have to do and the constant pressures of doing more, we find ourselves frustrated and stressed, wishing there was a magic wand to get organized and get it all done! Well, I am unaware of the creation of any magic wand, as of yet. I promise I will keep looking and let you know when I find it! Until then, let's look at the benefits of being more organized and a few false beliefs that may be standing in your way of having more time, reducing the clutter and creating a more organized life.

If there is no incentive, then it is easy to talk ourselves out of doing things. If we take the time to understand and connect with some of the common benefits of being organized, it may make it easier to add getting organized to our To-Do or task lists. I personally think it needs to be the number one, top priority item on the list; in other words...do it first!

Getting organized can be beneficial in various ways. I am sure some of these will resonate with you, and you can probably add many of your own to this list:

- Become more focused
- Manage your time more efficiently; be more productive
- Reduce clutter, enabling you to find things when you need them

- Reduce the number of last-minute time emergencies
- Reduce stress levels
- Look more professional, presenting a more positive business image
- Prioritization of your tasks
- Have increased peace of mind and a more balanced life
- Be more creative and energetic
- Have MORE time to do more of what YOU want to do

We all have problems, and most of those problems are caused by false beliefs. We can have false beliefs about ourselves, about others, and about emotions we may harbor or entertain. These false beliefs get formed and stored in our subconscious during the course of our lives. They will cause us to act or NOT act, because we are convinced or buy into the fact that they are true.

It is true some of us are naturally more organized than others, but anyone can learn to be organized. I don't want to dismiss the fact that it may also be more difficult for very creative people to get organized, but they can if they so choose.

Sometimes people use this as an excuse for being extremely unorganized, messy, frequently running behind, and always having drama in their lives. Yes, these types of things can cause havoc in your life; but it is not because you cannot be organized. It is because you have either convinced yourself (false belief) this is true or you really don't want to change. It could also be you just don't really care if you're organized or not.

So be honest with yourself and ask the hard question...

Why am I really unorganized? If the answer is you choose not to be organized and you really don't want to change, than that is okay. My suggestion is don't waste your time finishing this chapter. Move on to a chapter that may make a difference in your life, organized or not.

On the other hand, if you are very creative or unorganized... for whatever reason... and you are willing to change your mind-set, then hopefully I can help you gain some insights on how you can start making a great impact on your life and those around you. You may find changing your way of thinking can give you more freedom than you ever had before.

First off, allow yourself to be you. If you have systems that seem like chaos to the casual observer, but work for you, don't just discard them because of public opinion. There's no reason for your sock drawer to be organized by color, type, and texture if it's not important to you. Even if you don't organize everything in your office or home, organizing the important things can give you more time and freedom.

Have you ever heard "a penny saved is a dollar earned"? Well, let's start thinking, "Minutes saved are hours gained".

So if you don't have a lot of time to get organized, let's look at how you can gain some time:

- Start with a small project, like organizing your medicine cabinet or your bookshelf. Accomplishing just one tiny goal can give you the motivation to keep going and eventually organize everything.

- Don't be afraid to work slowly towards your goals. Take small steps; break large pieces down. Think about the next action that needs to take place, not the end goal. By breaking down your projects into the smallest steps, you won't get so overwhelmed by the large projects.

- If you are a "let's just do it" person, I suggest scheduling a day of non-interrupted time to organize your office. It may seem like a lot of time wasted; but just think of how you will feel, how great it will look, and how easy it will be to find things. Work from a game plan. Only 15 minutes of planning will save 60 minutes of unproductive time. Of even more importance, think how much more productive you will be in just a matter of hours.

- Recruit family or friends in an effort to organize your home. Partner up with a co-worker to get your office done. Hire a professional organizer or a coach. Having accountability and someone else's insight is time and money well spent. *Remember the benefits.*

We now know you have the time, so what is stopping you from getting organized? No more excuses, just do it!

Have you ever said: "Why bother; it will never work"?

My first question would be, "How hard have you really tried"? No one ever said change was easy; and if they did, they were wrong. Old habits don't have to be erased; they just need to be replaced with new ones that work for you. Trying to make a change can involve failure, but failure is really progress in disguise. If something does not work the first time, try revamping and making changes. It really is about finding what works for you.

It is so important to change your mind-set to believe life can be (and will be) better with some hard work and perseverance. I love the quote, "Thoughts become things"; and I truly believe, with a positive attitude and a belief in ourselves, we can do anything we want.

If not for yourself, take a few minutes and think about how being unorganized is affecting others. Try reaching a compromise in your life by organizing areas affecting other people or those that have given you problems in the past. If you're usually late for meetings, try creating a calendar system for yourself. Don't just assume your lack of organization doesn't cause any problems for those around you.

It's great when you find a system that works for you. Some people think they work best in an atmosphere of chaos; but if your disorganization spills over to affect other people, you may need to adjust your thinking. Do you pay bills late? Do you frequently forget appointments or show up late to functions? Is your home an inviting place or one your friends and family can't really feel comfortable in because of disorder?

Developing a positive mind-set is one of the most powerful life strategies there is. Change your mind-set; change your outcome.

Remember you don't have learn to get organized all on your own. Helpful tips are available on www.TheProductivityExperts.com

Seven Points of Impact

Point

6

Healthy Bodies
Alive to Thrive

About the Author

 Karen Garcia is a writer, editor/ proofreader, and transcriptionist. Her business, **Transblogger 4 Hire**, provides services for time-starved professionals.

Karen still plans to "thrive to 105" and hopes you will join her on the journey by subscribing to her blog at: www.thriveto105.com.

You can contact Karen at:
Karen@transblogger4hire.com,
kg@thriveto105.com,
or visit her website:
www.transblogger4hire.com.

Take a Deep Breath!

You Have Healthy Options

By Karen Garcia

January 14, 2010...a day that will live in infamy! Well, okay, maybe that's a bit of an exaggeration. But it is certainly a date I am sure to never forget! It's the date I heard the surgeon inform me that the lump in my breast was malignant...cancer. Few people are ever ready to hear that diagnosis; it never crossed my mind that it was even a remote possibility for me.

Most people close to me know that one of my goals is to live to be 105. I even have a blog titled, "Thrive to 105" (www.thriveto105. com). I've always been remarkably healthy...no serious illnesses, no broken bones, no hospital stays except for my babies...and I've always prided myself on living a lifestyle that would afford me the longevity I'm looking for. I love life, and living another 50+ years is something I look forward to with great anticipation! So how could this be happening to me?

As my daughter sat with me in the first surgeon's office where I was referred, he explained how they would cut into my breast, remove the lump, then perform the biopsy. At that point, my question was would they do the biopsy while I was "under" and, if it was malignant, remove whatever else they needed to remove? The surgeon's answer was, "No. If it's malignant, you have to come back for another surgery". Well, it didn't make sense to me that I should have to go under the knife twice, so I opted to get a second opinion. Little did I know this was the first small step on a journey I had never expected to take.

January was supposed to be an exciting time for me! I was moving into my own new apartment after a divorce and many months not having a place to call my own. As it turned out, my move date ended up to be two days after my biopsy. Instead of deciding where to put things in my new place, I was worrying about how to deal with a potentially life-threatening disease.

I believe that things happen for a reason...in a divine order, so to speak. This journey I am on right now is an amazing example of just that. As events unfolded, I realized it wasn't any accident that I made a new friend in the fall of 2009 through a referral from someone I'd never even met. It wasn't just a coincidence that I was made aware of a specific breast surgeon while in the process of my diagnosis that caused me to seek a second opinion. It was definitely a "God thing" that I just happened to open a container while unpacking in my new apartment and found a book I didn't even remember buying titled, Making Miracles. In it I read true-life stories of remarkable recoveries by terminally ill patients.

Rewinding back to that fateful day, I met with the second surgeon one-on-one and was given my treatment options, dependent, of course, on further analysis of my biopsy. Those options were:

- Lumpectomy
- Mastectomy
- Chemotherapy
- Radiation
- Reconstructive Surgery

I watched as diagrams and words were put on paper for me, and the matter-of-fact delivery of it all left me feeling very numb. Leaving the office building, I walked in a "fog" to my car and called a dear friend who lived close by, inviting myself for a visit and a good cry. As I lied on the bed curled up in a ball, I felt all those reactions you're told you'll have when dealing with a crisis or loss…denial, anger, sadness, fear. It was hard to know which feeling to give in to.

As the fog in my brain lifted, I headed home. While driving, I dialed that new friend of only a few months (thank God for the old and the new) to tell her the diagnosis I'd been given and the treatment plan that had been spelled out for me. Her reply to me at that point is also something I'll replay in my mind whenever I recall the events of that day. She told me, "Take a deep breath. You need to know those are not your only options".

What? I have options? How do you know? Who said so?

With a little guidance from this new friend to websites where I could find information about alternative treatments and clinics where those treatments took place, I began to research my options, quickly becoming my own patient advocate. I not only searched out websites, but I began to read: *Making Miracles* (Dr. Paul Roud); *Getting Well Again* (O. Carl and Stephanie Simonton); *Knockout* (Suzanne Somers); *The Breast Stays Put* (Pamela Hoeppner); *Outsmart Your Cancer* (Tanya Pierce); *Cancer Free, Your Guide to Gentle, Non-Toxic Healing* (Bill Henderson) and *The China Study* (T. Colin Campbell). It soon became apparent to this "information junkie" that there is so much more that cancer patients should be made aware of in regards to their treatment options and their healthy recovery.

What I found was information on what I can do as a cancer patient to proactively affect my recovery without having to choose the standard of care treatments offered by mainstream surgeons and oncologists. What I learned includes how stress, hopelessness, and repressed emotions can stimulate cancer cells and how impactful the mind/body connection is in recovering from cancer. What I am learning more and more about is the hugely important role that nutrition plays in alternative treatments and cancer recovery. Something as simple as the knowledge that cancer cells thrive on insulin can be of great benefit to those of us fighting to rid ourselves of this disease; yet it's not always likely you'll hear allopathic physicians discussing a change in diet as a way of improving your survival chances. I've drastically changed my eating habits, eliminating sugar and limiting animal protein in the foods I eat.

After weeks of reading and researching, I chose not to have surgery, undergo chemotherapy or radiation. It just didn't make sense to me to put chemicals in my body that would compromise my immune system while needing a healthy immune system to fight the disease. I also chose to leave the tumor alone, deciding not to disturb the original cluster of cells, taking advantage of other alternative treatments that will, hopefully, kill off the cancer cells without hurting healthy ones.

Exercising, working to control the stress in my life and keeping a positive outlook are all a part of my alternative route to cancer recovery.

The message I most urgently want to share with those of you with cancer that are reading this, or those who have loved ones with cancer, is to be sure and inform yourself about your options. Don't be afraid to ask questions and do your due diligence. The more you read and research, the more you find to read and research… and the more information you will find about healthy options!!

Let me interject here that I understand there is a place for the standard of care treatments; and people who are survivors, having used those treatments, would say they are "healthy" options. I won't argue that point with them. The end result for each individual is what's important. Choosing to go against the status quo in dealing with a scary adversary, such as cancer, doesn't work for everyone; and knowing you're doing so can make those around you uncomfortable. Just months after my diagnosis, my daughter-in-law's mother was also diagnosed with breast cancer. Her choice of treatment was a double mastectomy, chemotherapy, radiation and reconstructive surgery. At one point, she told me that she knew she couldn't do what I'm doing. Interestingly enough, I felt the same way about her choice. I couldn't accept having parts of my body surgically removed, followed by doses of chemicals with difficult side effects, then six weeks of radiation every day. Some say I'm courageous and some probably think I'm crazy. Some days I feel fear and worry, but most days I feel confident and strong.

Think of *me* as your new friend. Before you do anything about making the important decisions that will impact your well being and future recovery from cancer (and many other diseases), I'm asking you to *take a deep breath!* Take a little time just to investigate the other options you may have; because despite what you are told by the vast majority of physicians treating cancer, you do have options that don't necessarily include surgery, chemotherapy and radiation. It's important to make an informed decision about your treatment. Treatment options aren't necessarily right or wrong. What must be weighed is what works for you and what makes you feel confident and comfortable about your chance for a full recovery.

About the Authors

We are Mike & Fran Grooms, owners and operators of HighPowerMagnets.com. We have been crafting, presenting and selling therapeutic magnetic jewelry for over 12 years. Like us, many of our customers wearing our magnetic jewelry have reported results and relief from pain in the head, neck, shoulders, back, wrists, elbows, knees, ankles, and feet within minutes, hours or in just a few short days. If you suffer from everyday common ailments, live with acute or chronic pain or want to regulate your immune system so that you can live a healthier, more active life, magnetic jewelry might be the answer.

Our jewelry is available in a variety of styles, colors, and sizes. It is hand strung and consists of hematite high-powered magnets (a rating of approximately 1,700-2,000 gauss in each magnet). We use only the finest quality materials available, including sterling silver, genuine Swarovski crystals, Swarovski pearls, tiger eye, cat's eye, and extremely strong elastic cording that will not lose its shape and is very difficult to break under normal use. Our designs not only look great, but make you feel great as well. Each piece is versatile and works with any style, casual or elegant.

Visit our web site at: www.HighPowerMagnets.com. At checkout, type in the code "7 points" and receive 20% off your entire order!

Magnets Work

By Mike Grooms

My name is Mike, and I was born an entrepreneur. As a child, I sold everything I could get my hands on. There was nothing I wouldn't sell—if I believed in it, I would sell it. At the age of nineteen I opened a tile and paint store. It was a success; I thought I had made it. Life was good for a young man.

Things changed about a year later. During the summer of 1965, along with three friends, I headed to the Ozarks to do some fishing. Unfortunately, we had a car accident that forever changed my life. I don't remember much about the accident, but I can tell you that it wasn't customary to wear seat belts back in the 60s. They tell me I was thrown through the "rag top" of the convertible when we were going around a sharp curve, and I landed face down in the mud. My air passages were packed with mud, and the ambulance workers could not find a pulse. They thought I was dead. At the hospital, they found I was breathing and off to intensive care I went.

I remained in a coma for four days. When I woke up, I had pain all over, especially in my neck. Later I found out two of my vertebras were crushed. Miraculously, my spinal cord was not injured. I would recover over time. My life would be intact, except for having to endure relentless pain. It was intense at first, diminishing over the years, yet still existing as a dull ache and burning feeling in my neck...a forever reminder of that horrible accident.

Living a healthy, pain-free life is probably the most desired wish anyone can have. For years, I thought that was an illusive dream. I thought that pain would have to be my lifetime burden to bear. But I coped, and life went on.

Years later I had four wonderful children. Life was good again, except for the nagging pain in my neck. My new wife, Fran, was also an entrepreneur. She had a steady job, but her passion was making jewelry for herself and friends. We began to sell her jewelry at arts and crafts shows on the weekends.

I became a bartender at a country club; and shortly thereafter, I developed carpal tunnel syndrome, along with the numbness, tingling and pain associated with it. Someone told me that if I wore a magnetic bracelet, it would help with the carpal tunnel. I was skeptical, but purchased one anyway. The money I spent on that magnetic bracelet turned out to be the best investment I ever made. Over a brief period of time, my carpal tunnel symptoms disappeared. I then bought a magnetic necklace and the pain in my neck subsided. As long as I wear the necklace, I have no pain.

I was so amazed by the outcome that I began to do research on the magnets and their benefits. I learned that magnets have been used therapeutically throughout the world for hundreds of years and that the gauss (strength/pulling power) of the magnet is important. For therapeutic usage, a hematite high-powered magnet with a rating of 1,700-2,000 gauss should be used. The strength of the magnets makes a big difference!

Studies and clinical trials have shown that strong magnets can quickly reduce swelling, bruising and pain, and can significantly speed up healing from bone fractures and surgical wounds. Take a look at what some of the experts are saying:

> *"They (magnets) have proven effective in more than 80% of patients. There's no doubt about it—millions of people can be helped from chronic pain by the use of magnets."*
> W. Bradley Worthington, MD, Former President,
> TN Society of Anesthesiologists

> *"This is not magic. We have tested magnets on more than 5,000 patients, and there is absolutely no doubt... the treatment works!"* Robert Holcomb, MD, Professor of Neurology at Vanderbilt University Medical Center

> *"This is a revolution in the therapy for muscle injuries, joint pain and posture problems. We have treated 4,000 patients with whiplash injuries by means of the magnets and cured 80 percent."* Dr. J. B. Baron, MD, Medical Convention at Baylor College of Medicine, Texas

> *"Our players have used magnets for two years, and they have proven to be an effective aid in the recovery of professional football's aches, pains and injuries."* Ryan Vermillion, MD, Director of Rehabilitation for the Miami Dolphins

Compared to other pain relief methods, magnet therapy has one major advantage. Both research studies and doctors agree that magnets have no side effects; so they can be used as often as needed. People seeking relief from pain without medication are flocking to the natural alternatives being offered, including magnetic therapy.

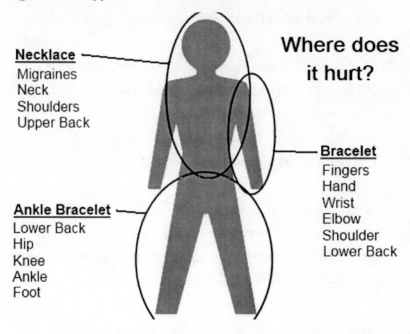

Where does it hurt?

Necklace
Migraines
Neck
Shoulders
Upper Back

Bracelet
Fingers
Hand
Wrist
Elbow
Shoulder
Lower Back

Ankle Bracelet
Lower Back
Hip
Knee
Ankle
Foot

Let's face it...all the research in the world pales in comparison to personal testimony, and I am living testimony to the benefits of magnets. As long as I consistently wear the magnetic necklace and bracelet, I am pain free.

As the cost of traditional health care is spiraling upward, I figured if we could provide a low cost/high quality magnetic bracelet that would help people, what a wonderful business that would be. So twelve years ago, we began to incorporate magnets into our jewelry. We didn't realize the impact we would have in so many people's lives. We followed our entrepreneurial spirit and began to sell our magnetic jewelry at arts and crafts shows and to businesses. Now, our website draws customers from all over the

United States! We have been blessed with a rewarding business that has helped thousands of people.

We invite you to try magnetic therapy to revitalize your energy... and enjoy every day of your life! We are so confident in what magnets can do. Simply wear our jewelry continuously for 30 days; and if you are not completely satisfied, return it and we will refund your purchase price. Visit our web site at: www. HighPowerMagnets.com. At checkout, when it asks for your dealer name/code, simply type in "7 points" and receive 20% off your entire order. Or you can call us at 1-800-310-3081 and mention this book for your 20% discount.

Thank you and have a pain-free life!

Acknowledgement: Caricature by Will Beard, Oxford, IA 52322

Disclaimer: We are not medical professionals but have been told not to use magnetic products as a substitute for necessary treatments. Never place magnets over an open wound. Individuals with internal or external electrical devices such as pacemakers, insulin pumps or defibrillators should not use magnets. Not recommended for use during pregnancy. Please consult with a health care professional if in question.

About the Author

 Maureen M. Wielansky owns Making It all Fit, LLC, a Health Coaching business where she teaches people how to heal their bodies and transform their lives. Although she specializes in assisting women, her services can be beneficial to anyone.

Maureen graduated from the University of Missouri in 1987 with a Bachelors in Psychology. She dedicated 20 years to her family, while working part time as a professional organizer. Maureen is an AFAA Certified Personal Trainer and has a Certification as a Holistic Health Coach through the Institute for Integrative Nutrition. Her passionate purpose is working with women, helping them heal their bodies so that they may carry the message of a healthy lifestyle to their families and eventually to the country Her mission is: To promote health and wellness through positive nutrition and save lives...one person at a time! You can reach Maureen and her team through: www.MakingItAllFit.com

You're Fired!
Now Go and Walk
this Miraculous Path!

By Maureen M. Wielansky

I always knew that laughter heals; perhaps that is why I intuitively see comedies when I venture out to the movie theatres. One of my favorite comedies, *The Blues Brothers*, contains a tongue-in-cheek sentence that sums up my life: "I am on a mission from God". My path to this actual purpose took numerous twists and turns with some great highs, some comedic segments and some near deadly lows. As I travelled my path, I let go of the weight of this world that was pressing down upon me. I also released 50+ physical pounds over the course of a year. However, in order to let go and go forward into the life I was destined to lead, I had to give up the struggle, surrender and fire myself as the CEO of my life.

The date of my firing: February 23, 2009. That's the day that changed everything. Prior to that, I was always so desperate to find the healing for my ills outside of me. I participated in numerous therapy, coaching and nutrition sessions hoping that they could heal me. One fateful day I was driving to see one of those healers when my "bitchy sissy" took over, telling me how useless I had become. My alter-ego berated me as fat, useless, and stupid. Food had become my best friend; but like a mean girl in middle school, food/my friend had betrayed me with physical illness and emotional instability. I began to dwell upon, and endlessly berate, my failings and shortcomings. I lied to myself, stating that I had failed in every aspect of my career, not only as a professional organizer (generating little revenue), but also as a wife, mother and friend.

My entire identity as "Susie Homemaker" seemed gone, since both my kids were away at school. I was carrying a major chip of resentment on my shoulder, often declaring everyone has done something to hurt me. All my manipulations and controls had failed to bring me true happiness. I felt responsibility for any pain my family had endured. In that moment of discouragement, I was told by the "bitchy sissy" that the world would be better off without me! When I heard that sentence, I had just entered a bridge. I knew a slight turn towards the water could stop the pain...but I didn't want to hurt the car. Yes, sadly, I valued my car over my own life.

When I arrived at my coach/mentor's office, I told her what happened. Then I cried, sobbed, dry heaved and cried some more. My coach just hugged me and assured me that she could see my greatness. ***But, for me to heal and recover, I had to shift my perception to believe I was worth it... that I was worthy of a miraculous life.***

I left my coach's office emotionally spent. I sought comfort in the only way that was familiar to me...through the consumption of food. I went to another one of a hundred fast-food restaurants that had provided me respite in times past. I binged, I wept, I struggled; and I vowed it would be the last time...then, I surrendered. I fired myself as the boss of my life and gave the job to someone who knew how to do the job better; I surrendered willingly to God.

Once I stepped down as CEO, miracles started to appear. The first came in the form of a support group with others like me. I shared my story, believing they would be horrified; but these amazing, big-hearted people smiled and nodded. They loved me enough until I could stretch and love myself. I threw myself into the program of recovery. I began to pray, read and journal. My body may not have been changing at that point, but my mind and spirit where clear and content for the first time since childhood. I allowed God to manage the rate at which my body was changing. I did the footwork and trusted God to take care of the outcome.

As the spring sprung and summer appeared, I became stronger. People around me started to notice my transformation. I started to burst out of my cocoon and took my rightful place as the butterfly.

Then another miracle appeared. My loving husband surprised me with a 30-day sabbatical at Hilton Head Health Institute. During those 30 days, I threw myself into the program of health and vitality. I attended every lecture and participated in three to four exercise classes a day. I ate six small meals daily full of fresh produce, organic proteins and whole grains. After the first week, I let go of 5 pounds.

Yet even more amazing was how I felt. My mind was clear; my energy was high and my skin translucent. My aches and knee pain disappeared. I fell back in love with running; but now it didn't matter that I was the caboose, I just loved the feeling. There was no competition anymore; it was all about participating and encouraging others.

At the end of 30 days, I let go of excess weight and found my passion: to help others feel as miraculous as I did. However, my vision was that they wouldn't have to leave their homes. I wasn't sure how I was going to do that, but then...another miracle appeared.

While at Hilton Head, I received a call from a Holistic Health Coach asking me to meet for a complimentary session. I met with every intention of working with her to further my progress towards establishing healthy eating habits. However, when we started to talk, my passion for others became apparent. She handed me a brochure from the Institute of Integrative Nutrition, telling me that I needed to become a health coach. Programmed in old responses, I immediately said, "NO", but promised to think about it.

The seed of desire was bursting forth in me. My gut was pulling me forward into the heart of my passionate purpose. I did my due diligence, researched online and talked to the great people at IIN (Institute of Integrative Nutrition). Rounding out my transformation, I honored that nudge and took a leap of faith... with God guiding me!

Today I am passionate about taking my mission on the road, letting people everywhere know that they can have health, vitality and energy; and it doesn't cost a fortune. If I can do it, anyone can. I emphasize to my clients that they have the power to heal themselves; and I am merely the teacher, facilitator, coach and cheerleader. I use my organizing skills to help restructure their kitchens and help them incorporate healthy choices in unusual, fun ways.

Being fired was the best thing that's happened to me. In surrendering my position of CCO (Chief Controlling Officer), I discovered my God-given purpose. It wasn't always an easy process, but the changes have saved my life. I share my story in the hope of helping others heal and transform their bodies and their lives. I want everyone to know that there is a better way to bring alignment into their physical and emotional wellbeing. We don't have to struggle. By focusing on areas of life that need balance, we are able to bring healthier eating patterns into our experience of life. By lovingly firing yourself as the boss, you open yourself up to miracles!

About the Author

 Brenda A. Fraser is an independent distributor for XANGO, a $2 billion dollar international health and wellness company. Her favorite products are whole-fruit Mangosteen juice, Eleviv for "vigor" and lowering her cortisol (the stress hormone), and Glimpse, a clean/green skin nutritional line that is certified toxic-free.

Brenda has been recognized as Colorado Business Council's Woman of the Year and was the 2010 "Beyond the Best" Business Award winner named by Streetscape Magazine. She was also recognized by Zonta International as the top recruiter of the year for attracting the most members out of 33,000 members worldwide.

Brenda is writing a book called "Building Abundance Fast", based on her model of cultivating customer and/or donor relationships. She resides in St. Charles County, Missouri, with her life partner. She still considers herself a Yankee at heart, having spent the first thirty-some years in New Hampshire and later, Washington, D.C. She can be found on Facebook, LinkedIn, and Twitter @GalaforceLLC or at: wwwmymangosteen.com/naturalforces or www.GalaForceEvents.com.

Help Is On The Way

By Brenda A. Fraser

I caressed my mother's hand and said, "Don't worry, help is on the way". Time had frozen in that moment of complete stillness. My car was sideways across a lane of traffic. One car had smashed into my front end, and another car had smashed into my driver's door. My leg was broken in multiple places, but I didn't know it. My ankle was severed, and I didn't know it. My ribs were broken, and I didn't know it. What I did know was that "love was all around"; because a cassette tape told me so, lying on its side in my lap, staring up at me, having been tossed from the glove box upon impact at the time of collision.

My mother died that perfect autumn day. Blue skies, bright sunshine, falling leaves...that day in October would change my life forever.

I found out later, she died at the scene. Although I had lived, I faced months of recovery from my injuries. I had two months in a wheel chair. There was a year of physical rehab; a year to contemplate the meaning of life and to appreciate my body, to learn to walk again, to go one full rotation on a stationary bike. I learned the value of friends who came to my house to build a wheelchair ramp. I learned the power of the phone to stay in touch with others and the importance of reading affirmations and positive books. The first one I read was called, "Spontaneous Healing", by Dr. Andrew Weil. Dr. Weil had a completely different approach to healing, nutrition and wellness. Unlike traditional doctors, Dr. Weil introduced concepts to me, such as holistic healing and taking responsibility for my own health and wellbeing. I learned that no one was going to do it for me. I had to learn to walk again. I needed to try new things, such as body massage and the use of therapeutic magnets; and I had to learn to eat differently.

"Thriving" is more than "surviving". Thriving means joy, happiness and inner peace.

A few years later, I was on a collision course to self-destruction. I was a binge drinker, a party girl; "work hard, play hard" was my motto. Despite a great career, lots of so-called friends, and a long-term relationship...I was dying inside. Worse than the physical consequences of a collision in a car was the destructive path that I was creating on a daily basis.

After a particularly demoralizing night following a black-tie gala to watch the Academy awards, I found myself naked in the shower, butt first, shower curtain underneath me, after I had fallen backwards into the tub while just walking into the bathroom. I'm not sure of the mechanics of that ordeal, but it wasn't pretty. The next day I decided to do something to change my life. It was too painful to continue the way I was living, although the other options weren't too exciting either.

After surviving the car accident a few years prior to this drunken Oscar night, I knew God had given me a second chance. Although I wasn't sure what that chance was all about, it certainly wasn't to end up a drunk!

After finding support and a program of recovery, I heard a wise man say, "Help is ON the way". His meaning was two-fold. First, I believe he meant "help" was coming in the form of spiritual guidance and protection through a "Higher Power". Secondly, "help" was other people—not doing it alone. Finally, "on the way" meant that the guidance we need comes on our journey, in small increments, from teachers, guides and others that God places in our life.

If you are hiking through the woods without a map or a compass and you come upon two paths...two choices...I believe God will either give you a sign to point you in the right direction or provide a person who has traveled the path before to tell you which way to go. At any rate, you do not need to know **exactly how you will get to your destination;** you just need to know that you need to be aware of "where your feet are" and be in that exact, precise moment upon the path. Your inner guidance system will steer you in the correct manner.

The most recent leg of my journey occurred on a snowy, pristine, New England night. It was a surreal night of peace and beauty. However, a phone call from my sister in Florida, telling me that my older sister in New Hampshire was suspected to be dead in her apartment, came like a loud and piercing scream to my heart.

It turned out that my sister had died of a sudden heart attack and had lay dead for three weeks in her apartment without any of her family knowing. You see, she lived a quiet and isolated life. Family lived out of state. Her grown and married children were hundreds of miles away; her grandchildren tucked into their little beds at night. No one knew.

To die suddenly is tragic enough; to die alone is even more profound.

What I learned from her death is written about in many women's magazines. The "Go Red Month" of February is dedicated to creating awareness around the vital signs leading up to a heart attack. If only my sister had seen these articles the month prior to dying. If only I had known. We didn't know that "flu-like" symptoms could be the precursor to a heart attack. Certainly, her weight was a contributing factor; and the cumulative effect of toxic prescription drugs she was ordered to take by doctors only added to her demise.

WHAT COULD I DO DIFFERENTLY to protect or prolong my life? I started learning what I could about nutrition, health and internal inflammation. I learned more about what foods to eat, how to exercise and maintain a healthy weight. I also started seeking out knowledge about nutritional supplementation. I learned that our food supply is nutrient deficient, that our store-bought meats are radiated, our foods over-processed, and that many toxins from food sources take a toll on our bodies over time. I learned that what we put in our mouths may only last a few seconds; but the long-term effects can cause damage to our hearts, our organs, and our internal systems.

As I started reading more nutritional-type magazines and books and seeking out information on the internet and at health/ wellness fairs, I learned that there are many companies offering products rich in anti-oxidants. But I found only one product that is rich in "xanthones"—powerful phytonutrients with unique health properties found in the rind of the mangosteen fruit. This purplish, tangerine-shaped fruit has been sought after since the Ming Dynasty throughout the Far East. There is only one "category-creator" product that uses the "whole fruit" in its entirety; that product is called XANGO juice.

Through reading about mangosteen, and meeting some of the doctors who have extensively studied it, I have learned that "help really is on the way". This time, the help is in an unexpected place —a bottle of delicious juice which, consumed three times a day, can reduce inflammation in my body and calm my symptoms associated with asthma (despite my love of my four cats, two dogs, and a bird). I'm now off my asthma medicine that I took for years, which was a steroid. I no longer take pain pills for my leg which I injured; and I can hike mountains in Colorado, walk the streets of Amsterdam or climb the stairs at historic landmarks. These things add joy to my life.

If you had told me that a shot glass would be filled with a health supplement someday, instead of what normally goes in a shot glass, I would have laughed. If you had told me years ago that I would understand the phrase, "help is on the way", I would not have understood. "A drink is on its way" was more my style.

If you are thinking about making a transformation in your life or changing the path you are on, whether it's to avoid a collision that is heading your way or to avoid a life-altering situation, you are not alone. Find a support group, find others who have "been there" and ask for help. Ask for directions. Seek answers. Empower yourself. Take responsibility for better self-care. No one is going to do it for you; but God will send you help along the way, if you trust, have faith, and take one step at a time.

About the Author

Angie Monko is the owner of Harmony Harbor, the Healthy Soul-ution (www.HarmonyHarbor.com). A resident of St. Louis, MO, Angie practices EFT (Emotional Freedom Technique) and is a Certified Hypnotist. As the "Soul Activation Coach", she specializes in helping women who struggle with weight, self-image and relationships learn to love themselves first, step into their greatness and then release the weight. She works with telephone clients from all over the country, as well as those local to her region.

Angie earned her degree from Southern Illinois University at Edwardsville in 1990 and spent 20 years working in the private business sector. Over the years, Angie realized she was more interested in helping others to heal themselves than focusing on company profits. As an introvert, she looked within for her answers. She soon realized she wanted to help others do the same thing. One day a friend suggested she look into life coaching. Through various referrals, she met a coach who lived one block away from her in St. Louis! This coach introduced her to Emotional Freedom Technique (EFT). On that fateful day, Angie fell in love with EFT immediately, because she knew it was her pathway to peace.

Angie has earned Advanced Certificates in EFT and Hypnosis. She now has her own coaching business, delivering awesome service to clients based on THEIR needs...to release weight, increase their energy and improve their relationships with God, themselves and others.

Healthy Soul-ution, Harmony's Safe Harbor

By Angie Monko

I used to think that being overweight was the cause of my unhappiness. Now I know it's the effect or painful symptom of my ingrained beliefs. I overate and used food to soothe myself and to quiet my anxious thoughts, because I didn't trust my soothing ability. I also used food for pleasure and comfort. I believed that I needed food for happiness, because I didn't subconsciously deserve and allow joy into my life. All of that has changed.

I've been overweight my entire life. Eight years ago I joined a twelve-step program that helped me tremendously to deal with the core causes of my food addiction. I still see myself as overweight. To this day, I retain an extra 15 pounds, although I'm confident this is changing. Up until I joined the twelve-step program, I was extremely unhappy with my body and often said derogatory things to myself. I obsessed over food and binged on sweets and salty food, hating myself even more after each episode. I learned that diets don't work. Even if I get to my goal weight, unless I've changed on the inside, I will regain the weight.

Yo-yo dieting left me feeling frustrated and hopeless. Counting calories or points and weighing frequently made me feel even more compulsive and deprived. By isolating with food, I created barriers to connecting with my true Self and with others. Responsibly owning my feelings was a foreign concept. I wanted to blame others for my pain.

I also saw in black and white, all or nothing, terms. If I couldn't eat or exercise perfectly, then I wanted no part of it. Scarcity thinking was my living room, the most comfortable room in the house, where I could bask in my "not enough-ness". Lack seems to mesh well with being overweight. I could never get enough food, because there wasn't enough time, money or love to fill the emptiness in my heart that resulted from self betrayal.

I had to get real with where I was. My results were like the elephant in the room. I can't deny them. They are my starting point. If I'm overweight, it's because that is what I want subconsciously. Sure, I know that I want to be slender and abundant consciously; but if that's not what I'm getting, then my much-more-powerful subconscious is dictating my actual results...often harsh, but always true. In my subconscious mind are records of everything that ever happened to me, which create my beliefs. They may be telling me that I don't deserve to release the weight and that it's not safe or possible.

As I question my beliefs, I see my insane thinking. I realize that I'm creating this inward battle and outward nightmare. I don't accept parts of me: my selfish and bratty teenager, my harsh critic (parent) within, and the part of me who gets overwhelmed and seduced by chaos. My emotions are a wonderful barometer of my core beliefs; and when those beliefs are threatened, I am fearful. When I come from a place of fear, devoid of self-love, I try to control everyone and everything around me.

My self image also plays a critical role in my success. I've always seen myself as chubby and frumpy. Being thin meant struggling with diets, feeling deprived, anxious and grouchy. Why would I want that? My job is to align my conscious desires with my subconscious desires.

I have sometimes felt like someone invaded my mind and took over my thinking. The ego self will always tell us we're not enough and that it is much safer to maintain the status quo. The ego's job is to keep us stuck, because that is safe. We have to learn to train and discipline the ego mind. We don't reject the ego, but we do relinquish it.

After looking at my belief systems, I had to decide: "Is it worth it? Am I willing to change? Is my pain enough that I will find a different path?" I reached my pain threshold in 2002 when I found my twelve-step program, but then I settled into a comfort zone. I have maintained my weight for nearly eight years. It seemed like enough. I thought it was vain to want a slender body. Now I realize that my "WHY" for releasing this extra fifteen pounds is much more than getting to my goal weight.

Who will I become in the process of releasing this weight? I will develop what I coin "The Soul-ution Mindset". It's no longer about perfectionism or needing people to approve of me. I can be successful and accomplish all I need at my current weight. So why do it? Because if I want to embody peace, love and joy, while being a role model for others who are seeking the same results, I must release the fear and choose love. When I release the fear, I release the fat. I'm not quite there yet, but I love the journey.

To achieve the Soul-ution mindset, I have to be willing to dispel my beliefs and mature. I take responsibility for my thoughts, feelings and actions. I blame no one. I live in the peaceful moment. I do one thing at a time, and I don't feel the need to rush or cram too much in. I trust God to lead me to the next right step.

My vibration determines everything that I attract. If I vibrate fear, I attract fearful circumstances. I've manifested this overweight body due to my inability to soothe myself without overeating. My thoughts and perception create my reality. My emotions impact my health and well-being. I might as well focus on what I want and stop playing childish games of illusion.

I have many Soul-ution tools that I use to help me on my journey to peace, love and joy. I use Emotional Freedom Technique, where I tap on energy meridians around the body to clear disrupted energy. I meditate daily. I practice ho'oponopono, a Hawaiian system of healing in which I say to myself, "I love you. I'm sorry. Please forgive me. Thank you." I pay attention to what I eat and drink and get plenty of water and exercise. Each day I perform a five-minute energy routine and practice Tibetan yoga rites. I write a daily gratitude journal and write about my feelings to keep myself aware. I study A Course in Miracles and pray and surrender daily. I practice Byron Katie principles and read, read, read. I also am a student of Universal Energy and practice this daily.

The Soul-ution results in my Soul Activation, remembering who I really am, my God Self Within. For the first time in my life, I have glimpses of, and communion with, my Soul. I am falling in love with myself. I am accepting joy, peace and love, which I've always blocked. As the result of knowing that God is my only Source and practicing faith consistently, I'm beginning to know freedom and reclaiming my life. I haven't reached any destination, because it doesn't exist. As I surrender to my lovely Self and accept me, in all of my splendid ego defects and glory, I am at peace. My life is perfect, and I am whole. I am SO grateful for this gentle understanding!

www.HarmonyHarbor.com

About the Author

 John Calvin Kluge (www.JohnKluge. us) is the husband of 7 Points Project Coordinator, Linda Fitzgerald Kluge. He is active in the New Thought and Holistic Healing communities and has enjoyed the benefits of Young Living oils for more than a decade. His passion is promoting health, happiness, helpfulness, and healing in the world through community service, balanced living and the use of therapeutic-grade essential oils. He has assisted many entrepreneurs in integrating the revenue flow from oils into their healing touch practices. He invites you to participate in the use of essential oils... to enrich your life and to make a positive difference in the world. To order products go to: www.youngliving.org/johnkluge.

Essential Oils Changed My Life

By John Kluge

My wife loves to network with other women...and often times they fill our home to capacity! So it was, in the summer of 2001, as I maneuvered my way through introductions at one of her gatherings, I came to meet three friendly and energized women, bearing 'purses' containing small bottles of essential oils. Laura, Mary, and Cris spoke excitedly about the countless benefits and "miraculous results" associated with personal applications of the world's purest floral and herbal essential oils. Since their enthusiasm was contagious, the oils caught my interest.

At the time, my knowledge of essential oils was limited to their use in scented candles and potpourri. I knew that aromatherapy was used to create a relaxing or romantic mood and fragrances could have powerful, unconscious effects on emotions and behaviors. However, most of my own experience had been with colognes and not oils. I recalled feeling embarrassed as a teen when my personal aroma of English Leather cologne turned 'stale' after a few hours of wear. This unpleasant memory and disastrous association with cologne and perfume caused me to hesitate when approaching the use of oils.

Over time I learned that there is a vast difference between colognes, aromatic-grade fragrances and the use of therapeutic-grade essential oils. I was accurate in my preliminary assumption that all oils are not created equal. There are many "rub-a-dub" and perfume-laden oils on the market for massage and aromatherapy.

However, with a variety of global distillation and packaging practices, we can find a wide range of oil purity, concentration, and safety. To fill more bottles and meet demands for lower priced products, the most precious and valuable oils are often thinned and diluted, drastically decreasing their effectiveness. More concerning is the fact that toxic carrier chemicals are being added to original oils by intermediate suppliers to make the formulation more commercially marketable, a practice contrary to the primary objectives of holistic health.

After weeks of listening to beautiful stories of "relief and relaxation"' from the use of "therapeutic-grade essential oils", I decided to see what they could do for me. Choosing where to start was nicely complicated by the fact that the oil source, Young Living Essential Oils, sold more than 200 options of single and blended oil formulations! Fortunately, to simplify my decision, a packaged combination of seven popular oils (Essential 7 Kit) was available over the Internet. It contained lavender, peppermint, lemon, and four 'theme' blends of 'Joy,' 'Pain Away,' 'Peace & Calming,' and 'Purification'.

To my complete amazement and delight, I discovered that massaging each of these natural oils onto my body created a remarkable sense of physical warmth, cleansing and satisfaction. Using pure virgin coconut oil as a natural carrier for the essential oils, my skin glistened; and unwanted skin tags and moles fell off. These personal results garnered my attention and became my own 'compelling testimony' to the use of oils.

I was beginning to see beneficial physical effects, while also having an increased feeling of optimism and well being! Making it even more appealing, I was beginning to look younger than my years.

Let's take a look at the oils I was using:

Lavender Oil – known as a calming and relaxing herb, frequently used for insomnia, anxiety, depression, and natural stress relief. One recent study discovered that the scent of lavender increases the time you spend in deep (slow wave) sleep. Other findings suggest that lavender reduces the severity of depression. Throughout history, people have turned to lavender to treat all kinds of ailments, including pain, headaches/migraines, muscle aches and sprains, burns, skin disorders, digestive complaints, allergies and infections. The most versatile of oils, because of its many healing properties, it is considered one of the best essential oils to have on hand.

Peppermint Oil – Is a sweet, highly fragrant essential oil with a long tradition of easing the digestive process, often used in massage to relieve muscle discomfort and credited by many to improve concentration. There are many recent studies showing the psychological power of scent, including peppermint's role in triggering positive sensations in the brain.

Lemon Oil – Citrus oils are now recognized for their powerful antioxidant powers, as well their refreshing and uplifting scent. They also support the body as a natural cleaner, deodorizer and sterilizer.

Purification Oil Blend – Is a cleansing blend of citronella, lemongrass, rosemary, melaleuca/tea tree, lavandin, and myrtle. Defuse this blend in homes, cars or hotel rooms to purify and disinfect your surroundings, cleanse the air, and neutralize disagreeable odors. It can also be applied topically to clean insect bites, cuts, and scrapes.

Pain Away Oil Blend – A comforting blend of wintergreen, helichrysum, clove and peppermint. Reduces everyday discomforts with a warming blend of oils.

Joy Oil Blend – Is an uplifting blend primarily containing floral essential oils such as rose, rosewood, jasmine, geranium, mandarin, lemon, ylang ylang flower and others. The essential oils in Joy are sweet and calming to the nervous system. A recent study by Japanese researchers showed that fragrance inhalation of rose oil show significant benefits, including a decrease in stressful adrenaline concentration. The alluring fragrance of Joy has an uplifting, positive, magnetic energy to which many women seem to be drawn.

Peace & Calming Oils Blend – Is a gentle, fragrant blend designed to promote relaxation and calm tensions. It contains the essential oils of tangerine, orange, ylang ylang, patchouli, and blue pansy. This powerful combination of oils calms and relaxes the body.

For the holistic practitioner, is there a debate over the use of essential oils versus fresh herbs? Well, there doesn't have to be. These things can have a synergistic affect on one's health regimen. Fresh herbs, citrus fruits and other organic products will always hold a natural place in the health enthusiast's diet. However, pure organic, therapeutic-grade essential oils, such as those produced by Young Living, contain concentrated amounts of plant herbs, are stored easier and last longer when distilled into the essence of oil. When ingested, they bypass the digestive system and are absorbed naturally into the body. Everyone, from infants to older adults, can eliminate the struggle to swallow capsules, as pure organic oils can be easily assimilated as a liquid ingested by mouth or through skin absorption.

Pure organic, therapeutic-grade essential oils are also cost effective to use, as they are one of the few substances on earth wherein the more you use them, the less you need them. For persons wishing to have a holistic approach to health, therapeutic-grade essential oils play a critical role not served by herbs alone or the lesser quality oil-based products.

Do the oils create 'miracles'? We are not giving medical advice here nor are we promoting exaggerated claims. Certainly many people, including me, have found pure-grade essential oils surprisingly effective in attaining positive results for health and wellness-related challenges. If one drop of peppermint oil can instantly bring relief to a sore throat, that's pretty impressive. If Joy oil can elevate your mood and positively impact your attitude, how priceless is that in your life? If peppermint can aide your digestion, panaway blend relieve pain, and lavender aid in sleep… why would you hesitate? Incorporating pure essential oils into my daily regime has forever improved the quality of my life…and I wish the same for you!

About the Author

Bridgette Kossor is a passionate advocate, teacher and inspirational speaker on plant-based/macrobiotic education, healthy eating and balanced self-love in people of all ages. She attended the Strengthening Health Institute in Philadelphia for Macrobiotic Education; and after many years of weight, body image and health issues, has shifted those challenges into positive action through her lifestyle choices, most passionately with music and food.

Bridgette is also a professional singer, songwriter, recording artist, interfaith minister, reiki master and "waker upper", well known for her dynamic, energetic and soul-felt performances. With a big and deeply strong voice that can belt out a powerful tune while delivering a loving whisper to your heart, Bridgette's love of music and people is joyfully contagious. "I feel alive!", "I feel young!", "I feel so good!", "I feel love", are regular comments that come from all of her audiences, young and old. Bridgette envisions a world where people are well nourished, aware, connected, loved, and co-creators of their own health and lives.

For more information about Bridgette, her music, performances, classes and "Feed Your Purpose" programs, please visit: www.bridgettekossor.com

Feed Your Purpose

By Bridgette Kossor

Purpose ~ Food ~ You... these three words, brought together in one place, are pure synergy... a powerful combination which unlocks the mystery to living well! What you eat, think and do all create the life you are living.

Purpose...the whole reason for your life on this planet and the driving energy behind what you do and why you do it. Purpose is the fulcrum, pivot or balance point of your "energy scale". Food, what you use to nourish your body, your mind and your spirit, provides the fuel or energy that makes the intangible tangible. Which brings us to...YOU; you are unique. Your purpose is unique; there is no one on the planet that can be and do you in the way that you are able to be and do you. Yes, I know. You don't think that you are quite so special and different or maybe you do, but are afraid to really live what you know to be true inside. Let's be clear right now. It doesn't matter what you do everyday, as long as you are being YOU, living your purpose and feeding it well.

What is a "purpose"? People have a tendency to think of their purpose as a mission or something they are meant to do during a lifetime. To me, our purpose is the energy and passion that "directs" what we do and why. Purpose drives our inner compass, which helps us to feel the energy of our choices. Simply put, if it feels good, it's a good choice, in alignment with your purpose. If it doesn't feel good, don't do it.

My purpose is to wake up, remember and celebrate the beautiful, sacred child I am...that child that we are, every single one of us. It sounds very spiritual, yet there is a playful, "feel good" aspect to everything I love to do and give. Children don't know they are spiritual in their minds. They innately are. So my job is easy. First, I do what wakes me up and helps me to remember that sacred being that I am; then everything I choose to do and give is celebrating, in a child-like, innocent energy. I get to play, as an adult, with child-like energy. Anyone who knows me can attest to the playful energy I bring to everything I do, along with the very deep spiritual remembrance. The most challenging part of daily life, for me, is staying awake and aware, so I can remember who I really am!

Can you see that without a connection to your own purpose, it's difficult to choose nourishment for your life or to know who and what you are feeding?

Let's talk about FOOD. What a ticking time bomb our concepts around this word can be...ready to explode...given all the taboos, labels, cultural influences, habitual patterns and baggage that it carries. What is food, really, but a source of fuel and energy? There is food for the body, for the mind and for our spiritual being. What we eat is affected by what we think, which is affected by what we believe. Yet, we continually research the physical aspects of food to isolate the "IT", the something that will help us lose weight, be healthy, thrive or simply not die. Yup...most of us choose what we eat so we feel a sense of security and well being. The simple days of eating to fuel our bodies have passed us by, unless we live in a tribe somewhere far away from civilization. We are afraid to be alone, because we are not comfortable with ourselves. We are afraid to die, because we are bankrupt in thought and spirit. These reasons for choosing what we eat really feed the fear inside.

There is no good or bad food. There is food that has life energy in it, and food that is dead (and I don't mean raw or cooked food). For instance, think of a tomato that you buy from a farmers' market in mid-July. Now think of a tomato that you buy from the grocery store in mid-January. Which one feels more alive to you? The tomato from July is more energized, of course. It came right from the life-giving vine, in the heat of summer, the perfect time to eat cooling and refreshing tomatoes.

This is how to choose your "food". What goes into your mouth becomes your new blood cells, which forms everything else in your body. What goes in your head becomes the thought that will direct your actions. What goes in your spirit becomes the belief that grows your life. Do you see why it is so important to have a directive inspiration that motivates you to feed all the aspects of your "self" in order to live your purpose? Don't eat or not eat something just to lose weight or be healthy! Just feel how incredibly limiting it is to feed yourself for something so small; really close your eyes for a moment, take a deep breath into your belly and feel what it's like to feed your greatness, for that is what your purpose is for you.

It is the bigness, the greatness, of your life that goes beyond any limits your mind may try to set for you when you don't honor your mind, spirit and body as a whole. Become aware of your thoughts, your body and your heart's passion. It is work... everyday. There is no getting around "the work". It's the best kind of work you can focus on. It is allowing the food to come into alignment with your authentic self and the hunger yearning within you. It is nourishment supporting your highest good. Just know and trust that you can get to the core of that authenticity through intuitive direction.

Now we come to YOU. Who are you? What do you love? These are the questions to ask yourself every single day, before you get out of bed and put your feet on the floor. Remember my purpose? It's always working now; wake up and remember that sacred child in you every day, so you can spend that day celebrating by doing what you love. You have learned to be who you thought you were supposed to be and do things that are expected of that person. Who are you, really, in that amazing body of yours? What does your spirit want to express by you being YOU?

I am in awe of the life I get to live. I love to sing, and through my singing I am living my purpose fully and joyfully. This also creates a way to connect with people, which just jazzes me, since I LOVE people. I also love to share new ways of eating, cooking and living in our bodies. This allows me to be with people and help people to wake up to themselves, which is an integral part of my own purpose. When we remember who we are and live our purpose, there is a joyful lightness to life. We feel free and loved, with an overflowing cup of love to share. This is everyone's birthright; and when you "Feed Your Purpose", you step up to claim that freedom of love.

Eat food that is full of life, think thoughts that are full of love, and believe in the truth of your spirit. That's it. When there are interruptions in this flow (and there will always be plenty!), just acknowledge them, feel it in the moment and come back to: "Who are you and what do you love?" It's like a deep breath of peace...

About the Author

Christine Anne, Family Nurse Practitioner. Christine's credentials include a Masters degree in Nursing, and a BSN with a dual degree in Child Development and Education. She has over 30 years of broad nursing experience as a staff nurse, Nurse Practitioner and Educator, including critical care, and family clinical practice. As a writer, speaker, and educator with training and experience in health care and natural wellness, Christine's educational programs have been authorized by the American Nurses Credentialing Center for continuing education credits (CEUs). Her broad-based education and experience has provided her the opportunity to work with all ages of children and parents—clinically in both medical and psychiatric settings, and professionally as an educator—as well as being an active community service volunteer. In a caring, unrushed setting, Christine's private practice provides wellness counseling, stress management, and gentle, healing therapies including Jin Shin Jyutsu, and Therapeutic Touch. In addition, Christine teaches courses on Touch-of-Healing Self Help, Personal Stress Management, and Self Esteem Enhancement, and makes presentations to groups locally and internationally about health and healing-related issues. Contact Christine Anne at 314-750-6876 or christine@christine-anne.com.

Slicing Your PIE of Life

By Christine Anne, FNP

Imagine that your life is a pie that you bake every day. Picture yourself looking down on a warm, steaming, fragrant cherry pie right out of the oven. As you look at your pie, your job is to slice the pieces into sizes appropriate to your daily Physical, Intellectual, and Emotional (PIE) needs. Each new day invites a new opportunity to bake a brand new PIE of Life, and slice it a different way.

Each piece of your PIE is an integral part of your life and health. Each piece requires some time, attention and energy on a regular basis. It represents one of the real and legitimate needs that interact to support your well-being. While each need is distinct from the others, together they cooperate and combine to flavor your life, just like cherries and juices enfolded in a flaky piecrust. To neglect any piece of your life's PIE will ultimately affect how the other pieces taste.

How can that be? It's because human bodies are composed of cellular, biochemical, energetic and neurological systems intricately integrated and connected. Each cell and system nourishes and is nourished by the others.

The beauty of this interconnection is that when you access and help one area of your life, you are accessing and helping all the areas. Energy is the common denominator that permeates and flows successively though every cell and system. So when you harmonize your energy, everything is being calibrated, balanced and stimulated for optimum health, healing and peace of mind.

To illustrate this finely tuned interconnection, consider this: You are driving 60mph, closely following the car in front of you. Suddenly with flashing red brake lights, that car comes to an abrupt halt. In a fraction of a second your whole body has been called into action. Your eyes see the car stopped in front of you. Your brain, having stored information about such events and how to respond, sends out an alarm to all systems. Their rapid response teams take instant action. Your body—with its own 24-hour pharmacy—starts pumping enormous amounts of chemicals into the blood stream to sustain the actions necessary for survival. In an instant, you are totally alert and present. Your mind is racing, heart pounding, eyes darting, breath gasping, foot stomping the brakes, hands tight on the wheel—all while your body braces and your ears anticipate the sound of a crash. A split second seems like eternity. You are flooded with emotions, fear, anger, grief or worry. This is your "fight or flight" response kicking in.

Can you see the interconnections? Your body is on-call to respond to every thought, emotion, sensory perception, or environmental cue. That is as it should be, but it can cause problems. For instance, when your body-mind perceives something as threatening, it responds accordingly—whether you are about to crash in your car or are simply late for your massage appointment.

Over time, strong emotions repeated daily, creating the fight or flight response, cause disruption, disharmony and ultimately disease by fatiguing the first responder organs as well as the cells that are being repeatedly flooded with stimulating chemicals and hormones. You can literally "stew in your own juices" because your PIE of Life has gotten out of balance.

You may be familiar with this disharmony. It manifests in headaches, back pain, ulcers, chronic fatigue, fibromyalgia, irritable bowel, cancer, depression, anxiety, sadness, low energy or estranged relationships, even your relationship with yourself. These symptoms can appear mild at first, but they will escalate if we neglect to bring our PIE of Life back into balance.

The three-step, triple-A recipe for bringing your PIE of Life back in to balance:

- Assessment
- Acceptance
- Action

Assessment allows you to see how you are slicing your PIE of Life and assists you in finding the cause of distress or disease. You can start with this assessment exercise, for which you will need a piece of paper and pencil:

Draw or trace a large circle putting a dot in the center. Like spokes on a wheel, write in the circle each of the 6 areas: Physical, Intellectual, Emotional, Energetic, Social and Spiritual. Look at each area and consider the time and attention it gets on a regular basis. For a more accurate visual image, draw lines from the center dot to the circle edge to slice your pie into the size of pieces representative of the attention given to a particular area. Don't think too hard about this; allow your instincts to prevail in this exercise.

Now look at how you have sliced your PIE of Life and allow yourself a few moments to identify your sense of satisfaction with how you are currently slicing your daily PIE of Life. Can you rate your satisfaction with a percentage? For example: I am 60% satisfied with physical care, eating, exercise, self care; or I am 90% satisfied with social life/recreation. Now in each slice, write your satisfaction percentage and shade in (starting in the center) each slice of pie according to your satisfaction percentage. How do you feel when you look at your diagram? If your pie turned on it's side to be a wheel, how smooth or bumpy would your ride of life be? Your pie gives you a visual picture, an assessment of the state of your life's PIE right now.

Acceptance, the second step in this process, means being honest with yourself and telling the truth about how your life is, without any shame, blame, excuses or accusations towards yourself or others. The simplicity of this can be reflected in the phrase "It is as it is." Saying this without judgment moves you towards acceptance. When you can admit there is an imbalance in your life without attaching judgment to what you observe, there will be enough energy and power of purpose to create the results you want in your life.

Defensiveness is a great clue that you have not come to acceptance. Denial and self-pity are addiction's best friends. Addictive behavior is to know something is detrimental to you or others in some way and continue to do it anyway. Ask yourself if what you observe in your life fits this description.

Don't worry if you cannot instantly come to acceptance. This can take a lot of personal processing work. Having a mentor or professional can be helpful making the process easier and faster. However you do it, though, you need to attend to the recipe with which you're creating your PIE of Life each day, so that your actions support health and peace of mind, and give you a smoother ride in life.

Action is the final step. Looking at your PIE, consider a place to start. Simple is best, so just pick out one or two imbalances and determine what results you would like to create in your life. It is best to start with an intention of how you choose to be. Your intention is like the umbrella under which your action choices will fall, i.e., in the physical slice, "I choose to be my ideal weight. The actions to do this will be to eat breakfast daily, or get some help with creating and sticking to an eating plan." Create new intentions as well as the corresponding actions necessary to fulfill those intentions.

Energy is vital to sourcing each piece of your life's PIE. Ways to balance and promote energy are a positive attitude, healthy eating, rest, fun and laughter, loving relationships, a sense of purpose, and even simple hands-on energizing exercises.

Each day as you climb out of bed, consider the gift of a new opportunity to bake and slice your PIE of Life in a way to nourish yourself and others. If you feel like you might need help with your personal recipe and how to slice your very own PIE of Life, give me a call. No one can bake or slice your PIE of Life for you, but when you reach out for assistance, you give yourself the gift of caring support and guidance, which can make all the difference between flowing or struggling through life. Life is just about learning and loving moment-by-moment and day-by-day. Savor the flavor and Enjoy.

Seven Points of Impact

Point

7

Flourishing Finances

Gladys Mercedes (Zamora) Schubach is the CEO/Owner of GMS Incentives, LLC, which offers promotional marketing solutions for companies globally. As a minority small business owner, Gladys opened for business in **Chesterfield, Missouri,** in 2002, with the mission of providing total customer satisfaction. GMS Incentives' philosophy is simple: Offer a wide selection of leading products at competitive prices and provide high-quality customer service via phone or email seven days a week. Their customers place orders with confidence, knowing they will be completed on time and accurately according to the high standards for which **GMS Incentives, LLC,** has quickly become known.

Gladys and her husband, Bill, lead and promote a healthy lifestyle through the use of Melaleuca health and wellness products. It is through their passion for helping people that they are taking one step at a time in achieving residual financial freedom.

Community service also plays an integral part in the Schubach household. Gladys currently serves as Vice President of the Zonta Club of St. Charles (2010-2011), part of an international service group to advance the status of women worldwide. She believes in empowering women by supporting and connecting them with the resources they need to succeed. Many St. Louis charities have been silently served through the heart-felt donations of GMS Incentives.

www.GMSIncentives.com

A Priceless Gift

By Gladys M. Schubach

The place: Miami, Florida; the year, 1962. My family and I came over as refugees from Cuba when I was just three years old. We had escaped from Cuba and from Castro's regime. Prior to coming to the United States, my parents lived a very happy and fruitful life. My dad, Ricardo Zamora, was the private body guard for Batista, the President of Cuba prior to Fidel Castro. After Batista fled from Cuba and Fidel became the new President, our family's situation changed for the worse. We lived in fear, not knowing what would happen to my Dad or to us.

My parents lived in fear for their safety and for the safety of their children. My mother, Teresa "Angela" Zamora, was very afraid anytime when school buses approached. The fear stemmed not from children being on the buses, but rather because the buses were filled with Castro's armed soldiers looking for people to take away—anyone the government thought was a threat or who was considered "anti-Castro". Also, in many places, there were spies who came in all sizes and all ages. We had to always be careful and never let our guard down. We were very fortunate to have been able to escape from Cuba and come to the United States in April, 1962.

We arrived in a new country, and we didn't know the language or customs. Thus, we had to start all over from scratch. I remember my parents were very frugal with everything; but in most respects, we didn't know we were lacking for anything. There were three children when we first got to Miami, and we lived with a family who was assigned to us by the American Red Cross. After a few months, our family was able to rent a one-bedroom apartment. My parents made sure to keep our cultural traditions alive and cook traditional meals for us.

We eventually left south Florida and moved to Chicago; ironically, to a neighborhood that was "All-American", i.e., no Hispanics in the immediate area. There was only a short time period when I felt "different" from the other kids at school. That was not due to my cultural background, but more so because my dad worked nights and mom worked days. Rather than eat in the school cafeteria, Dad always picked me up from school to take me home for a homemade lunch he had personally prepared. I guess my parents wanted to make sure that I ate a balanced meal or perhaps this was part of his traditions, born from his own heritage. These were special memories with my dad.

We didn't go out to restaurants or the theater. The setting for our entertainment was centered on us...talking, playing Dominos or Bingo. Fun times didn't involve money, but shared experiences and true intimacy with family members. For relaxation, we would go to the local park to watch the birds and just be in nature. These simple acts were so rewarding. Just having our freedom was pure luxury.

The key lessons I learned from my parents was the importance of family and that money didn't buy happiness. They were always affectionate and always reinforced our confidence with positive words, such as "you are so beautiful" or "you can do anything". Sometimes the things we say to our kids are the most valuable things we can give, the most priceless gift.

It's not where you go or what you do that is important. The important aspects of life are about appreciating the moment and being together. The simple fact that you are able to be together... that is the miracle. I never felt a lack of anything, because my parents made us feel "rich" in the intangibles. We didn't have a big home, but we had what money COULDN'T buy; our freedom... and it was priceless. Just having family was so important. My friends at school had some more materialistic things, but I never felt the void.

Everyone in my family worked together to achieve our goals; we always did what we needed to do, unconditionally. I am very thankful for how my parents raised me and my brothers and how we were taught to appreciate what we had versus what we didn't have. These values have always carried through in my life, especially in my business. I'm always willing to help people with their needs and look to continually build on relationships. I feel that when you have these ethical, solid values, you will grow from within, which will inevitably carry over into your professional life.

Being the mom of three daughters and a minority small business owner, I'm an advocate for supporting and encouraging women; however, both men and women should reach for their dreams and achieve professionally the true passions they have within. Financial freedom will be achieved with true focus and consistently pushing that door open. Don't allow any hurdles, whether small or big, to come between you and your goals. Define your vision and your mission, whether this is for a new business or an existing one.

Most of you will never know the hardship of being a refugee. Take heart! Don't be afraid to "start over" and maximize your resources by collaborating with other individuals or businesses. It's important to know that as a TEAM...Together Everyone Achieves More!

Our mission is to embrace what life presents us and always turn it into a positive. Buena Suerte Siempre....Good Luck Always!

*****

We invite you to connect with Gladys and her team at: www.GMSIncentives.com.

About the Author

Bob Baker is the author of *Guerrilla Music Marketing Handbook, 55 Ways to Promote & Sell Your Book on the Internet, Unleash the Artist Within*, and many other books. Get access to Bob's articles, ezine, blog, podcast, and video clips at: www.FullTimeAuthor.com and www.TheBuzzFactor.com.

Pooki Lee is the founder of the Gateway to Agape Choir. Her forthcoming book is called *Happy, Happy! Joy, Joy! 101 Ways to Live a More Passionate & Playful Life*. Learn more about Pooki and the choir at www.PookiLee.com and www.GatewayToAgape.com.

Do What You Love...
the Money MIGHT Follow

By Bob Baker

If the title of this chapter seems familiar, there's a good reason. I've taken the liberty of paraphrasing the title of a popular book by Marsha Sinetar, called *Do What You Love, the Money Will Follow*. I've been aware of this book for many years and have always loved the premise behind it: A persistent focus on doing something you are passionate about will lead to financial rewards, as well as personal satisfaction.

I feel blessed to report that I do, indeed, make a good living by engaging in things I love. These activities include writing and publishing books on marketing and self-promotion for musicians, authors and other creative people. I live a full and rewarding life —and I'm on a mission to inspire and empower others to enjoy the same thing.

But not that many years ago, things weren't so rosy...

Throughout my 20s and 30s I embraced the "Do What You Love" philosophy...in a big way. I played and sang in rock and roll bands, wrote original songs, and even released a couple of music CDs. I did stand-up comedy for several years and performed in, as well as directed, many local theatre productions.

For a 10-year stretch, I enjoyed my most ambitious project at the time: I published a local music magazine in my hometown of St. Louis, Missouri. I also hosted a local music video TV show for a few years; and in 1992, a small company in San Diego published my first book.

Throughout this era of my life, I had a blast doing things I loved. The main problem during these years was a serious lack of cash flow. I convinced myself to believe fully in the Do What You Love, the Money Will Follow concept. But as I eked out a living doing all these fun things (while enduring several not-so-fun temp jobs), there never seemed to be a sufficient amount of money following me. In fact, I mentally turned around often to see if more money was creeping behind in the distance. While a certain amount did trickle in (enough to provide a place to live and a working car), the abundance I heard so much about in the self-help books seemed to elude me.

The good news is, I finally figured out how to make the Love-Money principle work. The year was 2000. It was a new century, and I was about to turn 40. The prior two or three years had been a low point in my adult life, as I went through a divorce and worked through digging out of debt.

By the beginning of the new millennium, I was working a day job in the corporate world and getting on firmer financial footing. However, instead of getting comfortable with a regular salary and benefits...my entrepreneurial spirit was re-awakened. I decided that being an author, speaker and teacher was where my destiny lied.

My primary focus became promoting myself and my books on the Internet. While I had been on the Internet since 1994, I hadn't made the best consistent use of it. So I vowed to get serious and immerse myself in spreading my message online. Progress was slow, but I soon saw sure and steady growth. I wrote and published more books, posted countless articles, built up my mailing list, attended conferences, got to know people in my chosen field, and worked it with a vengeance.

Every year, my book revenue grew. I started saving money and looking ahead to the day I could support myself 100% by doing this thing I loved. That day came in early 2004, when I gave notice that I would be leaving my job to work full-time from home.

Every year since, more opportunities have come my way. I know it's a result of the many years I have dedicated to my core topic: Giving musicians (as well as writers and other creative types) the tips and tools they need to effectively promote themselves.

Over the years, I've also had the good fortune to meet and correspond with hundreds of people who have found a way to make a living (or at least substantial extra money) doing things they love. Most of these successful people embody some common characteristics – which I'll share with you in a moment.

I've seen these same traits come to life in someone very close to me—namely, my S.O. (Significant Other), Pooki Lee.

Anyone who has ever met Pooki knows she has a magnetic spark. She can light up a room with her energy and sense of joy; but, as she now admits, for years she didn't know how to use that charismatic quality for a greater good. Like I did in my 20s and 30s, she floated from interest to interest. She also chased money-making ideas based on the profit potential instead of what was in alignment with her true gifts (and who hasn't been guilty of that?).

But something changed in 2008. In June of that year, Pooki and I attended a service at the Agape International Spiritual Center in Los Angeles. It was founded by Rev. Michael Beckwith (seen in the movie The Secret, on Oprah and on Larry King Live). Attending that service was a powerful experience for both of us.

Not long afterward, Pooki attended an Agape Music Symposium, led by Rev. Michael's wife, Rickie Byars Beckwith. At this event, Pooki got the inspired idea to start a choir in St. Louis…and the Gateway to Agape Choir was born.

Pooki has had good ideas many times over the years, but I have never seen her take an idea and run with it like she has with this choir. It's been an amazing thing to watch; and since I was recruited to be the choir's Music Director, I've had a hands-on, front-row view of the journey.

As the choir has grown in St. Louis, so has Pooki's relationship with the Beckwiths and the Agape community in Los Angeles. It has been inspiring to watch her go from positively affecting a small group of people in her hometown to now making an impact with hundreds of people across the country.

Pooki is taking the next step in her evolution by developing an online presence that will help many people live a more passionate and playful life.

Here are four lessons I've learned from these stories of personal growth:

1) Everything you've ever done in your life has the potential to serve you now. Little did I know that the skills I developed in my 20s and 30s would be put to use all these years later. But those prior experiences gave me a rich set of skills I employ on a regular basis as an author, speaker, book publisher, and Internet marketer. Embrace and appreciate all the things you have done to this point in your life.

2) Choosing a focal point for your actions can be powerful. When I made the decision to finally focus my efforts on books and music marketing, I gained traction in a specific area instead of spreading myself too thin. The same thing happened when Pooki devoted herself to creating and developing a choir. Concentrated attention to a specific mission can pay big dividends!

3) Your success lies at the intersection of your unique passions and gifts...and a need or hunger in the world. Simply loving something and doing it isn't enough to bring a steady flow of financial abundance your way. For starters, you must be really good at the thing you love doing. Then, that thing must satisfy a need or solve a problem that many people have. They must also be willing and able to pay for it. In my case, I help artists overcome the confusion of promotion and sales. For Pooki, her gift is helping people feel joy and live a more passionate and playful life.

4) The money follows when what you love to do is tied to a greater mission to help others. The "Do What You Love" philosophy can backfire if you put too much emphasis on the "You" part of the equation. You should certainly love whatever activities you engage in, but your motivation must be rooted in serving others through your unique gifts and abilities.

When these four attributes are put into play, I believe the money can and will follow when you do what you truly love!

About the Author

Cyndi Brown is a highly successful business owner, motivational speaker, business leader and coach. She started her first business over ten years ago and managed its growth from inception to incorporation. Throughout the years, Cyndi hired, trained and mentored managers and staff in support of her business. Others naturally seemed to gravitate to her, and Cyndi found herself expanding her circle of influence to become a trusted leader within the business community.

In ten short years, the business became so successful that she is now able to devote her time and energy to coaching other women who want to live the life of their dreams. She is a loving, wholehearted, confident woman who willingly shares her wealth of knowledge and experience for the benefit of others, so they may accelerate their success beyond expectations!

Working together with her clients, Cyndi coaches using her unique "S-A-V-V-Y Goals System" to identify and add clarity to their goals, making them more attainable. She helps align those goals with her clients' unique natures, focusing attention on their passions and strengths.

Connect with Cyndi as Your Success Coach at:
www.EmpoweringU4Success.com

From Dish Rags to Riches:

Life Enrichment through Successful Actions

By Cyndi Brown

For years people have told me to write a book, telling others of my story "From Dish Rags to Riches". I thought it would be bragging. I thought it would be self-serving. Only after I was invited to write for an inspirational anthology book did I realize that holding back my story would be selfish of me. In fact, we must all share our stories of triumph and tribulations for the purpose of leading, guiding, empowering and inspiring others.

My coaching practice, Empowering U 4 Success, is designed for women by a woman who has walked a mile in their shoes. I am that woman, and this is my story. My intention is to show women that no matter where you came from or what has transpired in your life, YOU can create the life of your dreams! It's a matter of setting goals and working on them one bite at a time...just like I did!

"Strong Savvy Women" have been a theme in my life. I was raised by a single mother, struggling to provide for five children. My father was not in the picture and provided no financial or emotional support. To say we were impoverished would be an understatement...but somehow my mother found creative ways to manage it all and take care of all of us.

Although we were clean, clothed, loved and educated, I always knew this was not the life anyone would dream of having. As a child, I always had friends who had everything I did not have. I hung around those who had more than I. This helped me keep the big vision that I could be more and have more. There was nothing that was out of my reach as long as I could dream!

Entering high school I had big dreams already formed for my life, and I was in a hurry to make them happen. I mapped out a plan to finish high school in less than the typical four-year program. It included studying hard, passing all my classes, and taking summer school each year. I would graduate early and be on the road to success.

But all was not to be as planned. During my 11th grade studies there was a road block! I had gotten pregnant and was faced with life-altering choices. After weighing my options, I formulated plans to go into a "Catholic Girl's Home", as they were equipped to assist me during this time of transition in my life. And, I was fortunate to have a lovingly family who supported my decisions, knowing I would have the coming months to clarify my plans.

My sweet child was born on May 17, 1980. This day represented a major crossroad in my life. I had to decide in favor of adoption or accept the struggles of a young, single mother. Either decision would have been acceptable; to relinquish her with love, acknowledging the difficult situation I was in as a teenager or formulate an alternate plan for our lives. I chose the second option! I did not give her up for adoption and came home a few days later with my baby girl, Carissa!

Nothing was going to stop me from being successful! I just knew I could do anything my mind was set upon! Still needing to complete high school, I enrolled in summer school and eventually graduated six months before my graduating class. I was back on my path to success, entering college in January, 1981, the same month I graduated from high school. I remember pushing the baby stroller in the snow to get Carissa to the babysitters! Nothing was going to stop me from manifesting the life we deserved.

That is the level of determination I want you to call forth in your life. Draw on that deep-down knowing that you can accomplish your dreams...one step at a time, one challenge at a time, one victory at a time.

You may be expecting my story to soar to great heights as I finish college, get a great job, etc. Although that would be ideal, my path of learning, growing and maturing into a "Savvy Business Woman" would take an alternate route paved with "true grit" and downright determination. Three years after the birth of my first child, my son Jaycee was born. By the time I entered adulthood at 21 years old, I was married and divorced with two children to support. For the next ten years I worked in a restaurant, managed to purchase a house and struggled to make ends meet. It would have been easy for me to throw in the dish towel and give up on my dreams, but life without luster was not my style; and my entrepreneurial spirit took over.

While working in that restaurant, I met a woman who introduced me to Mary Kay Cosmetics and the concept of direct sales marketing. Interestingly, it was the fact that I could earn a car that captured my initial interest. My dreams began to come alive again. I left my job of ten years to earn a car! I did it within one year, because I had goals all along the way! Never underestimate the power of visualizing your dreams and setting goals to attain them.

Following my success in the direct marketing field, I opened my own company, A Living Angel Home Care Ltd. We help seniors stay in their homes, as an alternative to going into nursing homes. My mother, Alberta Brown, was the inspiration here. All my life, strangers have told me how special my mom is. She has taken care of seniors all her life. With her inspiration, love and encouragement, A Living Angel's concept was developed. We had a vision, worked towards the dream, set goals, and adjusted our course when needed. Our expansion came naturally, hiring reliable managers and a dependable staff. After a decade, we were so successful that I was able pass on the roles and responsibilities to a full-time manager and "retire" from working in a traditional manner.

Throughout the years, women entrepreneurs would call me asking for my advice. I mentored many women on how they could open their own businesses. We met to discuss "the next right step" for them to take on their paths. Sometimes we focused on business; other times we formulated personal goals for them to attain. I started the discussion and helped them dream big to set S-A-V-V-Y Goals. Over the years, many women have said, "Thank you, Cyndi, for that cup of coffee that made me believe in my dreams!"

So when retiring in 2009, I knew there was more for me to do! How could I help people and still help myself?

Throughout the years, I have often been coached. I could not have reached this level of success alone! In order to help others, it was important that I determine what I do best. The answer: **I inspire and help women!** Women just like me...Savvy Business Women! Thus, Empowering U 4 Success was established to help other Savvy Women live their dreams, through goal setting and designing the life they desire! The Empowering U 4 Success coaching techniques were developed from a natural gift I have for mentoring women and modeled after the goal-setting techniques I employed.

Empowering U 4 Success Teaches S-A-V-V-Y Goals
S-Sophisticated, A-Attainable, V-Virtuous, V-Valuable, Y-Yearly = SAVVY Goals

- Sophisticated – Complex, worldly, advanced, knowledgeable, up-to-date
- Attainable – Able to be accomplished or achieved with effort
- Virtuous – Moral goodness or righteousness; grounded in your values
- Valuable – Having importance, usefulness and great monetary value
- Yearly – Annually occurring

Mind Your Ps & Qs During the Process
- Ps = Produce Steadily, manifesting through set goals and actions
- Qs = Quantify Systematically, measuring your actions and results

Reach out and get help with the process. We suggest you journal on your "S-A-V-V-Y Goals", join a mastermind group, network regularly and hire a coach! Nothing replaces the one-on-one, focused support a dedicated coach can give; and he or she can help you mind your "Ps & Qs". We are available to help at: www. EmpoweringU4Success.com.

About the Author

Kelly Alcorn is 'The Business Activation Coach.' As a speaker, coach and mentor, Kelly works with individuals and groups to help them first identify obstacles and then create an activation plan that's life transforming. Kelly's unique approach inspires people to dream about and identify their goals; then she successfully moves them to action so they become successful achievers.

If you are an entrepreneur, solopreneur, service provider or sales professional and are "stuck" in one or more areas of your business, then it is time to schedule a business strategy session with Kelly. During the session, Kelly will help you get to the root of your challenges and provide connections and resources to get you back on track. The session will be followed up with a personalized action plan detailing what you can do to move powerfully in action towards your desired outcome.

Kelly earned her Bachelors of Science and Business Administration degree at the University of Missouri-Columbia and remains an avid lifelong learner. As The Activation Coach, Kelly offers cutting edge business coaching and personal mentoring to her professional clients.

Kelly is active in board membership and leadership support positions for several local chambers and organizations. Kelly was a top ten nominee for the Spirit of St. Peters Award and was recognized by Zonta as a woman of leadership in the community. Kelly is available to speak, facilitate your event or provide one-on-one coaching. Connect with Kelly at: www.KelltyAlcorn.com.

Passionate Purpose
Profitable Business

Ready, Set, Activate!

By Kelly Alcorn

You wake up and jump out of bed, excitedly looking forward to all you have to accomplish today. Is that how you start most of your days or are you like the many who drudge through the week looking forward to the weekend? Can you imagine loving your job, creating income from your God-given talents? If you have that inspiration, if you are drawn to that vision, then you are in the perfect place! I will show you a process you can use to discover and profit from your passion. First let me tell you a bit about my story and how this process came into being.

I was in the mortgage industry for over 10 years; and as Charles Dickens would say..."It was the best of times, it was the worst of times." I had created a six-figure income and loved helping families finance the American dream. I felt I approached the loan process with clients more from an educator's or economic strategist's perspective, showing how to purchase a home with the best loan that fit their income. I was happy. I was being helpful. I was solidly on purpose...and then shifts beyond my control began to occur. About halfway through my mortgage career, the industry went through some major changes; and the company I loved was "bought out" by a major industry player. Seemingly overnight, my whole world changed!

In reality, it took some time for the economic impact to be fully realized. My business dropped to less than half of what I had done the year before. For the next five years, I struggled to rebuild the business, but to no avail.

My finances were out of control. My savings had run out; I was living off credit cards. I grew to resent the mortgage industry and hated going to work. I remember telling friends I would go get a new job if I just knew what job to go get.

At the peak of my frustration, I went to a retreat where we defined our values, vision and personality style, with the intention of aligning with our true purpose in life. Based on what I discovered about myself and what I loved to do, it came to me that coaching was my God-given purpose. I was put on this earth to educate, motivate, encourage and guide others in their business endeavors...just as I had educated and guided people through the mortgage process. Only now, the scope of my offering would expand to be focused on assisting entrepreneurs and businesspersons.

I remember sitting in that room and sharing with my group that if I could do anything, it would be coaching others; but I was afraid I would not be able to pay my bills. Then it hit me; in recent years I had not effectively been paying my bills with my mortgage job anyway. Why not do what I love? I felt the fear of change and moved straight through it. I was tired of being unhappy...tired of feeling unfulfilled. I made my mind up that nothing would get in my way.

By working my way through my own career transformation process, I developed a coaching technique called "The Passion Process". In the Passion Process, you identify your passions, assess your skills, embrace your values, clarify your vision, and activate, activate, activate! Of course, we can only talk about the highlights here; and it flows better with guidance and mentorship, but here are a few of the keys:

Your Passions: Grab your journal, a notebook or open the laptop. List all the things you love to do. It does not matter if you think you can make money from them. Do not censor anything; put it all down. I have found it can be helpful if you do this exercise with a partner. Keep asking yourself, "How do I like to spend my time? What do I love to do? What do I find interesting?"

Your Skills: Next you will list your God-given talents and skills. What comes easy to you? What have you received praise or recognition for accomplishing? A great way to expand this list is to email those that know you well from work, volunteer positions or networking groups to see what skills and talents they see in you. Take time to notice which abilities are repeated and if they resonate with you.

Your Values: Identify your five core values. Start off by listing all values that matter to you. Your list should have at least 25 values noted. Next, go through the list and ask yourself, "If I could have just one, which one would it be?" Once you've selected that value, compare it to each and every value on the list and determine if it is, indeed, the absolute number one value. Continue to compare and rank them until you have your top five values defined. These are the "five core values" that will become interwoven into the essence of your business.

Your Vision: Examine your passions, skills and values. What income could you create from pursuing your passion utilizing your skills and living from your values? If you are having a challenge determining what job or business fits, you may want to call in the help of an expert. Sometimes we are too close to the situation, and someone from the outside can easily see how all the pieces fit together. Once you have a big picture idea of your new income source, create your vision statement. You could write a letter as if you had lived most of your life and detail all that you are appreciative of. You could write out the details of how you would like your life to be in one year. No matter which approach you take, the important thing is to be very specific. Where do you live and with whom? How do you spend your work hours...your play hours? Do you travel? What car do you drive, etc.?

Activate! Activate! Activate! Are you excited? Can you feel the energy of how amazing it is to live your purpose from your passions? I hope so! The next step is to activate your vision. Notice what comes up for you. Are you ready to move forward? Do you feel fear or hesitation? If you do, don't despair—that is quite normal. To move through this space, you can collaborate and create allies. You could do this alone; but the road is likely to be hard and lonely, and you may become susceptible to discouragement. I recommend you form strategic alliances, network with other entrepreneurs, hire a business coach, find a mentor, consider participating in a mastermind group and get all the support you deserve! It's time to value your vision, believe in yourself...and invest in your dreams. We are not talking reckless abandon here, but rather a comprehensive plan for success. For me to transition from the mortgage industry into my coaching business, I actually did a combination of all these things. I needed and deserved the components from each area to be able to create the business I envisioned. The same is true for you!

Remember:

- Identify Your Passions
- Access Your Skills
- Embrace Your Values
- Clarify Your Vision
- And... Activate, Activate, Activate

Connect with me if you'd like support through this process: www.KellyAlcorn.com

About the Author

Currently living in St. Louis, Missouri, with an undergraduate degree from Lindenwood College and MBA from Maryville University, Kelley Green has an unyielding drive to help others, especially with their finances. She discovered her true passion and opened Financial Housekeepers in 1997.

Kelley helps small businesses, independent contractors, not for profits and individuals achieve/maintain financial integrity and realize their goals through her consulting services. Kelley's team helps implement fiscally responsible action plans and provides support services helping clients reach their goals. They believe that now is time to start a movement, to provide financial integrity and peace of mind one bill...one financial obligation...at a time.

www.FinancialHousekeepers.com

Money Matters

By Kelley Green

Money matters...it really does. Money...it means so much and affects us so deeply, that often we do not realize our own issues surrounding finances and the subsequent consequences these issues have on our lives. The way we approach the handling of our money can impact the success of our businesses, our relationships with others, and our own feelings of self worth in profound ways.

I'm Kelley Green, "Money Maestro", and owner of Financial Housekeepers, a full-service payroll and bill paying company. Over the years, I've sat down with hundreds of clients and helped them develop a new approach to managing their money. Let's face it... money, and how we manage it on a daily basis, is one of the single most impactful areas of our lives; and there is no "Money 101" class to help us figure it out. Although I have consulted with many business owners, our emphasis is on money matters outside the business arena, in homes all across the nation. For as we heal the home, we also heal the economy.

Most people that I meet with are overwhelmed by their financial situation and don't realize why. So, where have we learned to manage our money? Typically from watching how our parents and our peer-class managed it. They have also helped program our comfort zone on money matters. Have you ever been asked what parish you live in or where you went to school? How about the kind of car you drive or where you work? These are social determiners that we ask each other every day. But what we are really asking is: Are we on common ground? People often tend to pigeonhole themselves and seek out friends who are financial equals to avoid feelings of discomfort or inadequacy about their own financial position. Succinctly put, people tend to do what is comfortable and embrace behaviors they have seen others model.

I met with one couple once who simply could not save money. Together they made over a hundred thousand dollars a year, but could not seem to save a penny. As we discussed the path that led them to their current destination, the wife recalled that when she was a little girl, she would save money. But when she went to get it, her father had taken it and spent it, sometimes on food for the family and sometimes on who knows what. She concluded that there was no reason to save money, because it would not be there when you wanted it anyway.

Her husband was the youngest of six children. His parents had lived through the depression. When his mother came home from the grocery store, she would go through each item on the receipt; and if something was even a penny off, they would go right back to the store and collect that penny. He grew up overly frugal with his money until he married.

Once this blessed union took place, each accepted their role in the "money matters". They decided that he would provide the bulk of the income, and she would take care of the household, including managing the finances. He assumed she would handle the budget to the same exacting precision as his mother. She had learned a different pattern. About five years into the marriage, the husband wanted to buy a new car; and when he went to get money from the savings account, it wasn't there. As you can imagine, this led to a huge fight, complete with accusations, counter defenses and, inevitably, hurt feelings and tears. The husband wanted to research where all of the money had been spent over the past five years, but the wife had kept no records. She felt unjustly persecuted, because all of the bills were paid on time, they lived in a lovely home and now he was yelling at her for not managing the money to his expectations. They each began to resent the other.

They could not see that their finances, their household and their relationship had been in the hands of first graders. One focused on knowing how each and every penny was spent and the other knowing that whatever was saved would be taken away. If you've met your inner 7-year old, you know that there is no reasoning ability there. Fortunately, they realized they needed help or this would have destroyed their marriage.

Getting to the core issues surrounding money matters and personal programming is critical. First you must get past the attachment to "how it was supposed to be". Once this expectation is released, the space becomes available to create a plan that works for each person involved. Secondly, clear concise communication is a vital part in this process. In the case of our couple, she agreed to keep track of spending; and he agreed to take a more active role in supporting her in saving for their future. They are now successfully saving money, have met with a financial investment advisor and are working together as a team and living like newlyweds.

This story is just one of many similar tales. We all have one, whether we are in a relationship or single. A lot of people are really bad at managing their money; and no matter how much they make, always want to blame their job or their chosen career. They think that everything would be just fine if they could only make more money. They deceive themselves when they think this way.

My parents are a prime example of how good money management can effectively work. They spent 30 years as elementary school teachers. Dad took on a hobby of restoring furniture, and mom tutored kids at our kitchen table to earn extra money for our family of four. Dad took care of the money. If we were lucky, we went out to eat once a week; but most meals were at home. We got school clothes at the beginning of the school year from the outlet stores—no brand names—and that was it for the year, other than an occasional outfit at Christmas or (God forbid) fresh off the sewing machine. I did not own a pair of brand name jeans or shoes until I was in junior high school; and as I recall, I had to pay for them. But guess what? Looking back, I had a great childhood. My parents were able to retire after only 25 years of teaching and are enjoying their retirement. My mom has a healthy appetite for shoes now; and from where I sit, she's earned every pair.

What is really important? What do you want your life to represent? When you look back on your life, what will be the things that really mattered? Will it be the beach house with the five-car garage or the laughter of your grandchildren as they play at your feet? Or could it be both? Take a moment and indulge yourself in an exercise. Close your eyes and picture yourself 5 -10 years in the future. Where do you live? What are you doing? Who is with you? How are you feeling at this moment in time? Are you filled with happiness or regret?

Now make a few notes for yourself about this vision. Is the path that you are currently on going to lead you to this future? If it is, congratulations; keep walking this path and don't lose sight of it. If it isn't, what changes do you need to make now to realize this future for yourself? What price are you paying for success? It really is up to you. It is not about luck. You make the choices. Life deals all of us a few curve balls here and there. If you need help dealing with yours, get an advisor... get a coach. Athletes are smart enough to have coaches, because a coach can see things that they can't see for themselves. A good coach can help you hit life's curve balls, find your path and help you reach your vision.

> *"It's good to have money and the things that money can buy; but it's good, too, to check up once in a while and make sure that you haven't lost the things that money can't buy."*
> –George Horace Lorimer, *Saturday Evening Post*

About the Author

Sharon Reus has launched a magazine, worked for two syndicated talk shows, interviewed professional athletes for ESPN and produced several national sales conventions for Anheuser-Busch. Her varied career spans more than 25 years; and all of her jobs have focused on persuasive storytelling, from both the journalism and marketing sides of the fence. Corporate clients of Sharon's have ranged from Volkswagen and BJC Healthcare to McCarthy Building Companies and the St. Louis Holocaust Museum. A graduate of the University of Missouri and Coach U, Sharon now functions as a producer, coach, facilitator and teacher, working with Fortune 500 companies and entrepreneurs alike, to help them create marketing and communications programs that get great results. Connect with Sharon on LinkedIn or via her website at www.SharonReus.com.

Top 5 Mistakes Entrepreneurs Make

By Sharon Reus

Business ownership can be exhilarating, rewarding and lucrative. But it's too easy for entrepreneurs to derail their own success by making basic mistakes in business management. Fortunately, these mistakes are easy to correct. If you see yourself in this list, take steps today to put yourself back on track.

1. Not Paying Yourself First

Perhaps the most critical mistake I see entrepreneurs make is paying everyone else before they pay themselves.

As a small businessperson, you probably incur expenses such as phone service, web hosting and tax preparation. You may also be working with partner vendors on projects, and they need to be paid out of your earnings.

Frequently vendors get paid first (because they're sending statements with big red stamps proclaiming "overdue"!); and the money that's left...what should be your salary...gets frittered away, paying for marketing, cost overruns and that gadget you can't live without.

It's essential to pay yourself on a routine basis—preferably once or twice a month. The amount really doesn't even matter, especially in the beginning. The key is to establish a regular payroll habit now and honor it. Determine how you will get paid. Will you write your own checks or have an accountant handle it?

Determine the amount and how you will handle taxes—quarterly, per check, and so on. (Check with your tax advisor for the best plan for you.)

When you don't pay yourself, you send yourself a message about your worth. As the head of your business, you deserve to be paid. No matter where you are in the life of your business, if you don't have a regularly scheduled pay system for yourself, set one up today. It's one of the most important statements you can make about your value and standing in your business.

2. Not Having a Clear Exit Plan

Some day you'll have to make a decision about selling, closing or bequeathing your business. That day is today, and here's why.

On a daily basis you make decisions about your business that affect its value. Which projects you accept, what investments you make, whether or not you hire employees—all of these decisions affect not only the day-to-day operations, but also the long-term viability of the business. If you know, for example, that you only want to work in your business for five more years, then you'll retire and shut down the business, that might affect your decision to invest in an expensive piece of equipment. If you're looking to sell the business in the next 10 years, you'll want to focus on building a profitable balance sheet.

Work with an advisor to develop a clear exit plan for your business. Of course, you can always change your mind; but having a plan on paper will give you peace of mind and help guide your decisions.

3. Not Being Willing to Sell

Picture a salesperson in your mind. What do you see?

Chances are you see someone very different from you. You probably have a negative reaction to the image. You may be thinking already, "That's not me. I'm not a salesperson". Selling has gotten such a bum rap over the past decades that most people are uncomfortable simply with the thought of interacting with a salesperson.

If you own a business, you're in sales. In fact, selling is your Most Important Job. If you hate that thought, you've got some work to do! The easiest way to enjoy selling is to change your mindset. You can view sales as a chore...a process in which you're convincing others to buy what you're offering...or you can approach it from the standpoint of making connections to find the people who need what you offer.

The most common barrier to effective selling is the fear of rejection. You fear being told "no" and think that "no" means, "I don't like you". Make the shift to remembering that you offer valuable services and products, and you're simply searching for those who can benefit from working with you. Then a "no" simply means, "It's not the right fit at this time"; and you can move forward with grace to talk with the next person.

It helps to tailor your sales and marketing process to your personality. Choose marketing venues that resonate with your skills and interests (public speaking, social media, article marketing, using direct mail, etc.) and the follow-up sales methods that work for you (phone calls, emails, in-person meetings). You'll be more likely to follow a program...and reap the financial rewards...if it feels comfortable for you.

4. Not Having a Board of Directors or Advisors

In the corporate setting, a Board of Directors is charged with protecting the shareholders' money and getting the best return on their investments. Ideally, the board helps direct the company's activities to ensure stability and growth.

A board of directors can be just as helpful to the small business owner. Even if you're not required to have a board (for instance, if you're an LLC or sole proprietor), you can assemble a team of smart, experienced businesspeople to help you brainstorm, create a business plan, make connections and get funding.

Not sure where to start in recruiting a board? Sift through your contacts to find people who have supported you in the past, other business owners and professionals in a variety of fields. Invite each one personally to join your informal Board of Directors. Hold two to four meetings each year to share updates on your company and gather input. Having an objective perspective will help keep your business on the right track.

5. Not Focusing on High-Level Tasks

Fortune 500 company executives share one important trait. They all spend the vast majority of their time focused on high-level activities, such as cultivating new customers, managing their company's brand and planning future initiatives. None of them schedule their own meetings, do their company's bookkeeping or take out the trash in the office at night. Some don't even know how to use email. They don't need to; they have "people" to do it for them.

Do you have people? Even if you're a "solopreneur", you can still hire virtual assistants or part-time professionals to handle low-level tasks. You're wasting your precious time and energy on non-revenue-producing activities if you're spending hours updating your website or sending out promotional emails. Commit to changing that tendency right now!

Most entrepreneurs say they can't afford to hire help. In fact, you can't afford not to hire help. Try this exercise: What's the biggest deal you've closed in the last year? What was it worth to your company? How long did it take you to close? A $10,000 deal that took you 10 hours over several months to complete means that your time can be worth $1,000 an hour to your company. How will you spend the next hour...wrestling with your calendar or connecting with your next client? Make the choice to leave the little stuff to someone else and spend your time on high-level, revenue-generating work.

About the Author

Cathy Davis is Creative Director and Managing Partner of Davis Creative, headquartered in St. Louis, Missouri. Davis Creative specializes in Business Identity and Brand Marketing, helping their clients DEFINE, DESIGN, & DELIVER a succinct and successful message to their consumers. Working in partnership with her husband Jack, they each have clocked-in over 30 years of branding, marketing and graphic design experience working for global Fortune 100 and Fortune "Top10" companies. Their global perspective allows them to utilize their macro-level insight to benefit their local, regional and national accounts. Around the corner, or around the world, they help their clients create a great identity.

Cathy is also the author of *"SeeMore Frog and the Midnight Flight of the CanBees"*, a motivational coloring book written in limerick format, for ages 6-106 (www.SeeMoreFrog.com). Readers of all ages come away with a smile on their face and a new-found sense of self-empowerment.

You can also find Cathy's humor and creativity at www.UPSIDaisy.com, where she plants Seeds of Positive Perspective. Choose from more than 50 original motivational and inspirational graphic illustrations, which can then be printed upon unique, one-of-a-kind cards and gifts for home and office.

DAVIS
CREATIVE

Cathy can be reached a: cathy@daviscreative.com or 314-374-7481.

Mindful Marketing

A New Way of Thinking about a New Way of Marketing

By Cathy Davis

There is a whole lot of talking going on lately about how to "brand" your business and/or how to create a "personal brand". It can be very confusing to new entrepreneurs or small business owners—especially when following the lead of "experts" only to end up with a business card and perhaps a website and no paying customers. So how can a business owner find their focus, follow their passion AND make a living—all while making a positive impact on society? By following the path of Mindful Marketing.

I've spent my entire career (30-plus years) in some form of Marketing, Advertising, or Promotion, working for well-known major corporations, on a local, regional, national and global level. I've learned a lot from the best of managers, and equally as much from the worst of managers. I've learned that it doesn't matter whether you are an entrepreneur working out of your spare bedroom, or a CEO working out of a boardroom—there are 2 primary components that all SUCCESSFUL businesses have in common—what I call Mindful Marketing:

1. Paying Attention to Brand
2. Paying Attention to "What Matters"

Let's break that down. *Mindfulness*, defined, is an in-the-moment, acute awareness of the pursuit of excellence. *Marketing* is making a positive connection with your consumer. *Mindful Marketing* is a way of doing business that leaves a positive impact on your bottom line—and is also a way of creating positive ripples with your staff, your vendors, your customers, and your community at large. At its core, Mindful Marketing is a matter of "doing what is right". When you add the concept of Mindful Marketing to your Brand Plan, you create a formula for success.

How Can Mindful Marketing Help Me Build My Brand?

Your brand is the foundation of your business. Your Brand is your Verbal, Visual and Virtual message that reaches everyone you interact with. More than your logo, more than your tag line, more than your website—your brand establishes the tone of how you do business and why your consumer should buy from you. Like a three-legged stool, your brand is built upon 3 "C's": Credibility, Connections and Consistency.

Establishing Credibility. Your credibility, or lack thereof, can make or break your business and your brand. Business credibility is based upon **Education, Experience** and **Entrepreneurial Integrity**. You may come to the table with multiple degrees from the best of colleges, or you may have taken the time to craft your talents and knowledge through the school of hard-knocks—either way, you increase your credibility factor when you follow the path of Mindful Marketing. As your prospects and customers see you taking care of what matters—by moving in trust, honesty and integrity—they learn they can trust you and your business. In times of economic instability, those consumers who are actually still making purchases are more likely to buy from businesses they trust.

Creating Connections. If you are a small business owner or an entrepreneur, you know the value of creating connections—also known as networking. Successful business owners do their homework before stepping out into the networking frenzy and can tell their business "story" in 60-seconds or less. Knowing the answers in advance to, "Who am I?" and "Why am I here?" opens the door to many successful (and profitable) conversations. Knowing your "story" and how you bring value to your consumer is the key to delivering your brand message. An easy way to remember your business brand message is to follow the WWWWW-H formula:

- **Who** is my customer?
- **What** am I selling?
- **When** does my customer buy?
- **Where** can my customer find me?
- **Why** does my customer want my product/service?
- **How** can I better serve my customer?

When you add the element of Mindful Marketing to your brand message, you tap into your customer's Predominant Buying Motive. Before your consumer can ask, "What's In it For Me?" (WIFM), you have already explained to them, "What I can Do for You!" (WIDU). Your consumer learns that you are here to help them—to offer solutions—to make their life better.

Maintaining Consistency. At the "end of the day"…"in the scheme of things"…(choose your metaphor), successful business brands pay attention to what matters most:

- Taking care of **PEOPLE** (self, family, friends, staff, vendors, charities)
- Staying "on **PURPOSE**" and following your personal mission and vision
- Sustaining a unique prosperous **POSITION** in the marketplace

- Living up to your **PROMISES**
- **PROMOTING** a product or service that fills the need of your consumer

When you take care of what matters most, and follow the path of Mindful Marketing, people want to do business with you. It doesn't matter if you are a one-person consulting agency or a global entity with thousands on your payroll, there are 10 primary common denominators that I have noticed that lead to brand success:

- **SERVE:** Offer a product or service that "serves" your consumer; find your niche, fill a void.
- **BELIEVE** in your product or service. Believe that you can make a difference and you will.
- **PLAN TO SUCCEED:** Set goals, make lists, take action, step off the cliff, MAKE A PLAN—Go beyond "Planning to Plan".
- **ESTABLISH** a business based upon trust, honesty and integrity.
- **FIND YOUR FOCUS:** Define your "position". What makes you (your product/service) bigger, better, smarter, faster, easier, etc. than your competition?
- **BUILD YOUR BRAND:** Shout your story from the top of every tree. Don't be shy.
- **CREATE VALUE:** Build positive relationships and rapport with your clients, your prospects, your network, your vendors, your staff, your community, etc.
- **GIVE** more than your consumer expects; be of service in the present moment. Call in the experts, play your strengths, re-frame your weaknesses.

- **FOLLOW THROUGH** on your commitments (to self and others).
- **LISTEN CAREFULLY, RESPOND PRO-ACTIVELY,** and watch your business grow.

We are entering an era where small businesses that invest in trust, honesty and integrity—the core elements of Mindful Marketing—are becoming the business leaders for tomorrow. Consumers today are more educated. They analyze their purchases and they want their purchases to make them "feel better". A great example of this is the Dove "Campaign for Real Beauty". Dove was inspired by a global report showing that only 2% of women felt that they were beautiful, and 81% strongly agreed that there was an "unrealistic standard of beauty that most women can't ever achieve". The Dove marketing campaign has proven successful because it challenges stereotypes and provokes ongoing discussion to support self-esteem in women. Women feel that Dove understands who they are.

Consumers don't want to be sold to, they want to be "in charge" of their purchases. The big brands of the past are giving way to new brands that appeal to a few rather than targeting the masses. Your brand—and your business—will succeed and fail to the extent in which customers identify with what you are selling. Which basically means they want you to be sincere, put your consumer first and be Mindful of why they should buy from you.

H-m-m-m-m...sounds a lot like Mindful Marketing.

An Invitation to
Connect & Participate

Thank you for being a part of our lives. We cherish our readers as new friends and look forward to serving your needs through the services offered by each individual author. Please connect with us at:

www.7PointsOfImpact.com

If you are an aspiring writer, published author, personal coach, business mentor, spiritual guru or everyday philosopher who has something inspiring to say, we encourage you to write in our anthology book projects! We believe in giving value to the reader, while opening an avenue for services and revenues for the participating authors. Our live events and members' website serve as a benefit to all who come seeking. Contact Linda Kluge for more details at: www.7PointsOfImpact.com

LFK Consulting
7 Points of Impact
P.O. Box 888
Bridgeton, MO 63044 USA

info@7PointsOfImpact.com

LaVergne, TN USA
15 January 2011
212316LV00005B/4/P